Hollywood DIGS

Micky Moore with Mary Pickford in Pollyanna, *1920.*

Hollywood DIGS

An Archaeology of Shadows

Ken LaZebnik

Kelly's Cove Press

Berkeley

Published by Kelly's Cove Press
2733 Prince Street
Berkeley, CA 94705
www.kellyscovepress.com

© 2014 by Ken LaZebnik

Published in the United States of America
ISBN 978-0-9891664-4-7
Library of Congress Control Number: 2014931284

FIRST PRINTING

Cover image: On the set of the film *Career* starring Dean Martin, Anthony Franciosa, and Shirley MacLaine, 1959.

Across from title page: Micky Moore with Mary Pickford in *Pollyanna*, 1920.

"A Leigh Wiener Gallery": All photos by Leigh Wiener.

"Samuel Goldwyn's Birthday Party:
A Contact Sheet by Leigh Wiener": All photos by Leigh Wiener, 1962.

Cover and interior design by Lynn Phelps.

Acknowledgments

While it is customary to save the greatest thanks for last, I will start with the one indispensable acknowledgement, because no one ever reads these things to the end: without Bart Schneider, this book would not exist. He suggested the idea, prompted the writing, patiently encouraged me, brilliantly suggested additions and deletions, and made sure each element of the production of the book was beautiful.

Devik Wiener shares the keen eye of his father, and has graciously given of his time and artistic insight to cull through thousands of Leigh Wiener's photographs and share with the world these remarkable photos.

Pepperdine University Libraries have provided invaluable research support and a home away from home. My deep thanks to Dean Mark Roosa; Head of Special Collections and University Archives Melissa Nykanen; Archivist for Special Collections and University Archives Katie Richardson; Librarian for Digital Curation and Publication Kevin Miller; and research specialist Beth McDonald.

Princess O'Mahoney generously spent time relating her father's saga with honesty and insight, and provided personal photographs that were deeply appreciated. Kathy Zuckerman spoke about her experiences with wit and wisdom, and has become a treasured friend who shares a love for stories about writers in Los Angeles. Norman Powell offered tremendous insights into his father's life and his own remarkable life as someone who has worked successfully in virtually every aspect of Hollywood. Tricia Newman and Sandy Kastendiek Drake shared their father Micky Moore's story and his extraordinary wealth of notebooks and binders filled with remarkable photographs. My friends Michael and Arla Campus contributed their great humanity and insights about our experiences working with Thom Kinkade. Shirley Jones was kind enough to respond to an inquiry about Samuel Goldwyn's birthday celebration.

For their technical and professional help, I am indebted to Brandon Scheirman, Julia Drake, and Theresa Rife. I owe a great debt to Pamela Espeland, whose editing was skilled, incisive, and challenged by my prose.

Lastly, and here I will bow to tradition in acknowledging at the end those who are most important: my wife, Kate, and our sons, Jack and Ben, have been endlessly supportive as I wrote this book. The time a writer takes away from his family can never be regained, and I am fortunate in having a family of artists and warriors who understand that following one's passion is an inner command that is ignored at one's peril. Kate, Jack, and Ben have my endless love.

Contents

1   Introduction

7   F. Scott Fitzgerald in the Butler's Cottage

19   Jock Mahoney: The Thirteenth Tarzan

31   Gidget, Alive and Well in Malibu

42   A Leigh Wiener Gallery

67   Elizabeth Allen's Garage Sale

75   The Dick Powell Show Grades Jack Nicholson: C+

85   Mel Shavelson and the Last Bugler

99   Samuel Goldwyn's Birthday: A Contact Sheet by Leigh Wiener

121   Providence

139   The Judy Garland Show

147   The Painter of Light

159   The Man Who Worked in Movies for Eighty-Four Years

171   A Neighborhood Walk

W.C. Fields in fur and derby.

Introduction

I WALK DOWN Ventura Boulevard every day, stepping over diamond-shaped plaques embedded in the sidewalk. Etched on the granite slabs are credits for films and television shows shot in Studio City: *The Pharmacist*, W.C. Fields, 1933; *Angels with Broken Wings*, Binnie Barnes, Gilbert Roland, Republic Pictures, 1941; *Family Affair,* Brian Keith, Sebastian Cabot, 1966–1971. One of my son's kindergarten teachers was a quiet, unassuming woman, extremely pleasant, who shocked us one day by casually remarking that she was Sebastian Cabot's daughter. Mr. French had a daughter? The gentlemen's gentleman from *Family Affair* was not actually a confirmed bachelor but had a daughter who is now a middle-aged kindergarten teacher? Such is life in Studio City.

The Studio City Walk of Fame is my community's heritage, a long granite graveyard of films and TV shows, memorialized like battles from distant wars. *Rawhide; With Six You Get Eggroll*; *Biff Baker, U.S.A.* This drumroll of American entertainment is usually the only physical sign that history was made here. Travel to Pennsylvania and you can still walk over the field at Gettysburg. In South Carolina, one can visit Fort Sumter. In Studio City, the lagoon where they shot *Gilligan's Island* was paved over for a parking lot.

Civilizations build upon the ruins of their predecessors, creating a layer cake of cultural strata. Archaeologists in Jerusalem excavate beneath debris from the 1948 war to a layer holding the remains of a seventeenth-century temple, then dig below that to remnants of a Crusade, then go deeper still to uncover shards of

Sebastian Cabot in derby, with (clockwise) Brian Keith, Anissa Jones, Kathy Garver, and Johnny Whittaker in A Family Affair, *1967.*

Roman history. Hollywood, too, contains material for an archaeological dig, but not of physical remains; the bulldozer of Southern California development plows too swiftly and deeply for that.

My stretch of Ventura Boulevard is within blocks of CBS Radford Studios, a charming little lot that began its life as home to Mack Sennett in the silent era, and then became the shooting site of many Depression-era Republic Studio films. Eventually CBS bought the property, and dozens of television shows have been shot there, ranging from *Gunsmoke* to *My Three Sons* to *The Mary Tyler Moore Show*. A second unit may have spent a day in Minneapolis, filming MTM tossing her hat in the air downtown, and getting the establishing shot of her apartment in south Minneapolis, but the show was taped in Studio City on Radford Street. As New York *echt* as *Seinfeld* felt, it, too, was taped at CBS Radford. *Leave It to Beaver* may live in our minds as the ultimate vague suburban U.S.A., but its home was at Radford. (And in the 1990s, an adult Jerry Mathers was a fixture coaching park baseball at nearby Beeman Park.) All those worlds—Dodge City in the 1880s, a New York City apartment, a Minneapolis television studio—have been struck. They have left behind just trace remains in the Los Angeles desert.

Pam Smith and Jerry Mathers in the Leave it to Beaver *episode "Beaver's First Date," 1961.*

This book is a series of Hollywood digs. By peeling back layers of show business, I hope to uncover a shared history, a story of American dreams. I begin with a physical location, but because what was once there has generally disappeared completely, my excavations will usually consist of a few artifacts. They are all that's left. More often, script pages and pieces of film denote a place and time without physically occupying the terrain. What remains of Hollywood are the individuals who held sway on these fleeting landscapes. These essays chronicle people who played roles large and small, but always significant in Hollywood: the stuntman, the screenwriter, the second-unit director, the great American novelist living in the carriage house of a film butler's mansion, Marlon Brando's makeup man.

If some of these figures are unknown, that's only fitting. Hollywood in both theory

Amanda Blake as Miss Kitty in Gunsmoke, *1966.*

and practice is a realm of make-believe, a civilization of shadows, which is constructed, lit, peopled for a few days, and then struck. Ultimately, it exists only on film and in the airwaves, transmitting phantoms that appear in our homes, and now on tiny screens we hold in our hands, the images indissoluble and yet completely without substance.

The history of film and television is a history of people who are gathered together, work with a single-minded fanaticism on a project, bond together—and then all go their separate ways. The sense of community is intense and intensely transient. Working in pictures is the joy of gathering a group of comrades in the sun, striving toward a highly finite goal—getting the film done—and then disbanding abruptly. Many have likened it to the army, to war, and it's the closest many civilians come to reenacting Sherman's march. A film crew is a voracious beast that descends upon a location; lies, cheats, and steals to achieve its goals; and measures success only in capturing the shot.

Film crews are analogous to Celtic warriors gathering for a series of battles, except that between wars, the Celts traveled with a clan. Between jobs, those who work in film are outcasts from their community, each an island unto himself or herself until the next job. I think that is why the biographies of Hollywood film people are so often chronicles of work and career, isolated from the city that hosted them. Like the gold-rush mentality that F. Scott Fitzgerald noted of Los Angeles, people come to Hollywood to dig relentlessly, not to build community. They leave behind shadows, traces of their past, which are quickly blown away in the heat of the next Santa Ana wind. This book is an archaeological dig for shadows.

This photograph of F. Scott Fitzgerald appeared in the June 1921 issue of The World's Work, *a year after Fitzgerald published his first novel,* This Side of Paradise.

F. Scott Fitzgerald
in the Butler's Cottage

I'M ASHAMED TO ADMIT that I graduated from college more familiar with the work of Edward Everett Horton than F. Scott Fitzgerald. It was the 1970s; nothing was required, and I sprinted through *The Great Gatsby* for American Lit. I vaguely remember our class discussing the significance of the green light at the end of the pier; we decided it symbolized money.

A glittering prose style should not be read between pinball games. In St. Paul, Minnesota, where I lived, there were dim resonances of Fitzgerald as an icon of elegance, and some scruffy Macalester College students would periodically troop down to his preferred bar at the Commodore Hotel, which remained a mirrored Art Deco wonder. I spent more time drinking in his romantic setting than I did reading his writing.

In contrast, I spent many evenings admiring Edward Everett Horton at the College Film Society. He played countless fussy butlers and functionaries in films from Hollywood's golden age. Like many character actors of the 1930s, he seemed to have just one character in him: the leading man's anxious sidekick, a blustering penguin whose trademark line was "Oh, dear." He played professors and valets, those two types essentially verging into one MGM standby: the ineffectual man in evening dress, high-falutin' and ready to be taken down a peg.

Horton's characters had names like Hiram Dilworthy, Mr. Witherspoon, Professor Reginald X. Shotesbury, and Ernest Figg. He made his bread and butter moving through a fictional world that mirrored the one Fitzgerald helped create: men in tuxedos, cocktails served up by a blustering factotum, dressing for dinner at the club—a universe antithetical to my galumphing, bearded, pot-smoking friends, stomping around campus in Sorrell boots and immense coats from Ragstock.

That was the attraction for me: a nostalgia for a fictional era I never lived in, where people seemed to have fun. Fun is investing yourself into an activity that you're keenly aware means very little and will produce nothing of importance, and the early 1970s took themselves with an earnest seriousness of purpose about everything. Tinsel on the tree was suspect.

Twenty years later, in the 1990s, a decade with nothing but tinsel, I moved to Los Angeles for the same reason Fitzgerald did: I had children to put through school. Hollywood is the place where the art and commerce of writing is neatly cleft, with the art thoughtfully stored away in an evidence bag, available for display at awards season. Everyone refers to making movies and television as "the industry" or "the business." Writers refer to their scripts as "projects," as in "I've got a project at Disney." The working vocabulary is an odd combination of advertising mixed with industrial research and development. Writers "pitch" ideas for "pilots." Networks strive for "tent pole" shows and studios yearn for "franchises."

Fitzgerald called Los Angeles a mining town set in Lotus Land: "It's a gold rush, and like all gold rushes, essentially negative." But he also knew this about life: "The test of a first-rate intelligence is the ability to hold two opposed ideas in mind at the same time and still retain the ability to function. One should, for example, be able to see that things are hopeless and yet be determined to make them otherwise."

Whether they know it not, this is the motto of most Hollywood writers. The tension of art and commerce creates a hopeless situation, and yet the best writers are still determined to create something beautiful.

Fitzgerald certainly tried to do this while he was out here. One would think that someone who made his money from spinning short stories for popular magazines would be able to conquer screenwriting. But Fitzgerald spent the better part of three years in Hollywood and ended up an outsider, without a contract, struggling to get work. He had just one onscreen credit, for *Three Comrades*. It was not a sole credit. The producer had assigned Edward E. "Ted" Paramore to write with him. Fitzgerald had known Paramore years ago in New York—and in *The Beautiful and Damned* had created a character named Fred E. Paramore who gets drunk and crawls on a living room floor whimpering, "I'm not a guest here—I work here."

In his notebook, Fitzgerald captured precisely Hollywood's scale of economy: "Junior writers $300. Minor poets—$500 a week. Broken novelists—$850 - $1000. One play dramatists—$1500. Sucks—$2000. Wits—$2500." One might note that Fitzgerald's weekly MGM contract paid him $1,000.

I find Fitzgerald's conviction that he could write for the Hollywood studios touching—we all like to believe that we can crank out a Hollywood hit—as well

Fitzgerald in 1937, the year he moved to Hollywood. Noted photographer Carl Van Vechten took this portrait.

Scott and Zelda in Dellwood, Minnesota, 1921.

as the honest application of his talents toward that end. He never seemed to understand he was throwing pearls before swine; or that, at the least, it takes a second-rate talent to successfully write second-rate assignments. He became romantically involved with a beautiful gossip columnist, Sheilah Graham, who grew up impoverished in London's East End and in Los Angeles reinvented herself, as so many others have done here. She claimed to be a British aristocrat, but Fitzgerald, with his instinct for uncovering character, soon understood her true story and took it upon himself to offer Graham an education of sorts.

As the story is masterfully told in *Intimate Lies*, the book Graham's son Robert Westbrook wrote about their romance, Graham once admitted to Fitzgerald that she had never read any of his writing. Scott said they would purchase his books that very evening. They left his room at the Garden of Allah apartment complex and walked along Hollywood Boulevard to the Pickwick Bookstore. Fitzgerald asked, "Have you books by F. Scott Fitzgerald?" The clerk replied, "Sorry, none in stock." Fitzgerald asked, "Do you have any calls for them?" And the clerk replied, "Oh, once in a while, but not for some time now." Graham suggested they try another bookstore. But it was the same story there.

Fitzgerald, as Westbrook writes, now had a grim determination to continue. He and Graham trudged in silence to a third bookstore, where a gray-haired man presided over a chaos of volumes stacked everywhere. He did not have any of Fitzgerald's books but asked which ones they were interested in. "'This Side of Paradise,' 'The Great Gatsby,' 'Tender Is the Night,'" came the reply. The proprietor promised he would try to get them and asked for a name and address. "I'm Mr. Fitzgerald," Scott said defiantly. The man reacted with shock and said he was very happy to meet him. But: "[It] was clear … why the old man had been so surprised when Scott had revealed his name; he had believed quite simply that F. Scott Fitzgerald must surely have died years ago along with his era."

Reading letters Fitzgerald wrote a couple of years after that event, I noticed the return address: 5521 Amestoy Avenue, Encino. Encino! For me, Encino is the neighborhood a couple of miles down Ventura Boulevard, a mélange of vast, soulless homes, mini-malls with expensive stores full of clothing you wouldn't want to be caught dead in, purchased by aging female realtors (my wife calls their bright red pantsuits spangled with decorative American flags "High Encino") whose husbands are paunchy white guys wearing pants with elastic around the ankles. It's the zenith of the Valley's bourgeoisie aspirations. Picturing F. Scott Fitzgerald in this milieu boggled the mind.

Then I saw a letter he had written to his daughter, Scottie, declaring he was living in a "cottage in the country." Of course. Encino in 1940 was still largely undeveloped; farmland and ranches. Fitzgerald's cottage must have been more like a writer's retreat than a suburban home. I looked up 5521 Amestoy in the *Thomas Guide* (once the true bible of Los Angeles, this thick book maps out the entire city). I drove to the address, hoping to find a little landmark forgotten by time. The street is residential, but as I approached 5521, it dead-ended, cut off by the 101 highway. It looked like the Ventura Freeway had buried the old cottage.

A few days later, I read this in a chronology by Matthew J. Bruccoli, the majordomo of the Fitzgerald industry: "October 1938. FSF moves to cottage on the Edward Everett Horton estate, 'Belly Acres,' at Encino in the San Fernando Valley." My God. Fitzgerald in the last year of his life, his book royalties dried up (all of his novels together earned less than twenty dollars in royalties in 1939), trying to write *The Last Tycoon* in between scrambling for freelance screenwriting assignments and churning out Pat Hobby stories for $250 a crack in *Esquire*, supporting Zelda in her sanatorium and Scottie in her college—this great American talent not only had to deal with those daunting tasks, but also had to face the daily humiliation of living as a tenant of Edward Everett Horton, comic butler, on his estate Belly Acres! I studied the *Thomas Guide* again. Yes. Amestoy dead-ended into the 101. But on the other side of the highway, a thin gray line showed a street running for a scant half-block. I drove there. I looked up and saw the street sign: Edward Everett Horton Lane.

Today it's all gone: the estate, the cottage, and the fields. Now there's an apartment building, monolithic, gated, quiet except for the hum of traffic along the 101. A check on the Internet revealed that Horton was dubbed the unofficial Mayor of the Valley, residing at his estate until his death, and this little half-block of a street is his permanent memorial. Sheilah Graham, the woman Fitzgerald was seeing in his last years, had rented the cottage on Belly Acres for him.

There is one resident of Los Angeles who remembers Belly Acres well: Frances Kroll Ring, Fitzgerald's last secretary. She wrote a book about the experience, *Against the Current*, a memoir of the twenty months she was "Scott's" secretary. He hired her specifically to work as his typist/secretary on *The Last Tycoon*, but she quickly became an invaluable part of his life.

Los Angeles is a vast town and forever surprising one as a small town. So it seemed both improbable and inevitable when I discovered Frances Ring is my friend Lucy Cotter's aunt. In television writing terms, this would be the third-act twist, the improbable and yet inevitable event that propels the story home into the fourth-act resolution. I looked to Frances Kroll Ring to be my "Morris the Explainer"—that character in a script who shows up to dish out backstory. Or, in this case, to flesh out the relationship between the great American novelist and the man who would later portray Indian medicine man Roaring Chicken on *F Troop*.

Frances Kroll Ring is smart, sophisticated, impeccably honest, the sort of person one hopes Fitzgerald would have assisting him in his final year. She was a native New Yorker whose father moved his furrier business and family to Los Angeles. Like newcomers through the decades, Frances found the neutron-bomb quality of the city disconcerting: street after street of homes, yet no resident was ever seen.

Because of the subject matter of *The Last Tycoon*, Fitzgerald wanted a discreet secretary with no connection to the studios. Frances is the soul of discretion. She looked aside at the gin bottles clustered in a desk drawer. Edward Everett Horton, however, was another story. Frances arrived one day to find Horton peering into the trashcan, fussily shaking his head at the pile of empty bottles. She approached him and asked, "May I help you?" Horton looked up, clucked his tongue, as he did at Fred Astaire in *Top Hat*, and said, "Looks like a case of the DTs." He waddled off, presumably to confer with his mother about the problem.

Horton once told a reporter, "I have led a serene life. I gave up all mental activity

Edward Everett Horton appears pleased with his hair product and dapper in pinstripes.

at eighteen." He was the son of a *New York Times* compositor, but his mother, Isabella, was the dominant figure in his life. Horton purchased Belly Acres in 1924 and moved his mother in. She resided there until her death in August 1961, at the age of 101. Horton was, in the vernacular of the time, a confirmed bachelor. He came to acting early and spent a lifetime working, from Broadway in the 1920s through the Astaire-Rogers musicals, through *Holiday, Here Comes Mr. Jordan, The Gang's All Here*, all the way until his final screen appearance in 1970's *Cold Turkey*. Horton said of his film career, "I never argue about a film. I just want to know how many weeks will it take and how much money will they pay." He also said, of acting on the stage, "A low trick I hate to stoop to is tying and untying my shoelaces. It seems to fascinate audiences … probably because so many women in the audience have their shoes off, or wish they did."

Edward Everett Horton was most successful at keeping his private life from Hollywood's view. Anthony Slide writes that he maintained a long-term gay relationship with actor Gavin Gordon, Garbo's leading man in *Romance*. For decades, Hollywood's rule of thumb was that anything was permissible as long as it was kept behind closed doors: homosexuality, alcoholism, stupidity. Let it out of the closet and the town would turn its back on you. It seems no coincidence that in Los Angeles every house is surrounded by fences, gates, and obstructions. Coming from the Midwest, with its wide-open vistas down block after block of unfenced lawn, I saw Los Angeles as it really is: chopped-up, every man's home more than a castle, a walled prison keeping the world out and the secrets within.

Edward Everett Horton created his own castle, Belly Acres, in secluded Encino. Enter F. Scott Fitzgerald, whose trademark was public revelation, whether it meant leaping into the fountain of the Plaza Hotel or writing about his *Crack-Up*. Now he tried to hide his problems (he dispatched Frances to dump burlap bags of empty gin bottles into the brush along Mulholland Drive, an episode which made its way into the Pat Hobby Stories). But he had already made a drunken fool of himself, and written about it, in the short story "Crazy Sunday." Scott tried to play the role of a gentleman, but one day when Horton appeared with some guests who wanted to meet the author, they found Fitzgerald on the stairs outside his second-story bedroom, tearing up planks of wood and hurling them to the ground. Horton quickly escorted his friends away, probably muttering "Oh, dear" as he went.

Horton was an actor. His job was taking on roles and interpreting a character. Fitzgerald was a writer, and a writer who believed that "all writing is swimming underwater, holding your breath." He worked on *The Last Tycoon* fitfully while at Belly Acres, between an odd screenplay assignment, Pat Hobby story, and occasional binge. Frances would arrive in the morning to find *Lost Tycoon* pages or a Pat Hobby story written by hand on lined paper the evening before. If it was a story, she'd type it and send it off to *Esquire*. Fitzgerald needed the $250. His contract with MGM up, he was desperate for money. Horton, meanwhile, was getting $2,500 a week for appearing in *That's Right, You're Wrong* with Kay Kyser and Lucille Ball. But Horton loved the theater, and he had a notion that provides me with an Act Four resolution, tying up the strings between all these lives.

The Pat Hobby Stories—comic shorts about a hack writer in Hollywood—were how I first got hooked on Fitzgerald. (They remain essential reading for Hollywood writers who wish to take an hour to wallow in depression.) Frances typed them. Edward Everett Horton was interested in creating a stage play out of them. Frances's brother Morton was interested in attempting the adaptation. Morton Kroll wrote to Fitzgerald, sending him some short stories he had written, and Fitzgerald wrote back with these words for a young author:

> A young writer is tempted … to be guided by the known, the admired, and the currently accepted as he hears a voice whisper within him, "Nobody would be interested in this feeling I have, this unimportant action …" But if the man's gift is deep or luck is with him … some other voice … makes him write down those apparently exceptional and unimportant things and that and nothing else is his style, his personality—eventually his whole self as an artist. What he has thought to throw away or, only too often, what he *has* thrown away, was the saving grace vouchsafed him.

Fitzgerald nourished his devils and was transparent. Horton was closeted. One was rewarded during his life with an estate in Encino. The other was rewarded only after his death with the fame he thought had slipped from his grasp forever.

As the character Pat Hobby in the stage play, Horton would appear as the bumbling hack screenwriter, fulfilling a role that his impoverished tenant created out of desperation. It might have worked, but the project was never realized. It's one of countless failed ventures that sit in boxes in Los Angeles. Edward Everett Horton was busy, anyway. Frances told me he was rarely at Belly Acres during Fitzgerald's tenancy. He was off touring the popular play *Springtime for Henry*. (Thus even Mel Brooks becomes a footnote in this story.) Frances remembers Horton's mother

Isabella, a cheery, grandmotherly figure, receiving packages from her son on the road. He often mailed her his laundry. Both our postal service and notions of what we expect from mothers have changed.

In May 1940, Fitzgerald moved to 1403 North Laurel in Hollywood to be closer to Sheilah Graham. I asked Frances if there was any dramatic scene as Fitzgerald left Belly Acres. Was there a memorable parting between writer and character man, a moment of fireworks between the author of *The Great Gatsby* and the actor who would later narrate *Rocky and Bullwinkle*'s "Fractured Fairy Tales"? Did Fitzgerald stumble out of the house, his old topcoat wrapped tight around him in the blinding San Fernando Valley sunlight, the damn heat and sun that never leave us? Fitzgerald always wore his old Homburg hat. I imagine their final encounter:

EXT. BELLY ACRES—DAY

In the verdant garden, Horton is directing his YARDMAN, a lithe young Latino.

HORTON: Be sure and deadhead the roses. They grow so much better when you treat them sternly.

Horton looks up. Fitzgerald is reeling across the lawn toward his car, a tiny, beat-up Ford.

HORTON (CONT'D): You off, Scott?

Fitzgerald turns back.

FITZGERALD: What's that?

HORTON: Nothing, nothing.

Horton stoops to tie his shoelace. A beat. Fitzgerald leans forward, looking on with interest.

FITZGERALD: Leave this place, old man. It'll kill you!

Horton glances up and takes a few steps back toward his home.

HORTON: Oh, dear.

FITZGERALD: Get out of Hollywood!

Fitzgerald picks up a potted plant and hurls it onto the drive. The clay SHATTERS. Soil scatters over the blacktop like loose change from a cracked piggy bank.

FITZGERALD (CONT'D): Good-bye, Eddie. I'm off to my paramour.

Horton does a double take.

HORTON: I didn't know you were a Methodist.

Fitzgerald stumbles into his Ford. As the car pulls out of Belly Acres, Horton waddles back into the house.

In a porch window, the silhouette of his MOTHER appears as she watches her son approach to tell her the story.

Frances Ring couldn't recall any parting scene. She remembers Horton as a penurious man, amiable but businesslike. He died in 1970, still on his estate, now memorialized with a lane.

Edward Everett Horton played a role in the fictitious world of RKO musicals, informed by the gin-drinking, carefree, madcap antics that Scott and Zelda incarnated. Horton acted his part and then came home to Encino, where he fit like a glove. He was a worker in the industry, and happily so. Fitzgerald was an authentic artist, the real thing, and he never found a home in Hollywood. There is no street in Los Angeles named after him. It wasn't his town. But I find Fitzgerald's year in Encino inspirational. As we all do, he struggled to support a family and write well at the same time—commerce and art wielding their endless tension. We all find ourselves residing on Belly Acres at some point, and we work through it as Fitzgerald's tombstone reads, quoting the last line of *The Great Gatsby*: "So we beat on, boats against the current, borne back ceaselessly into the past."

Jock Mahoney as Tarzan in Tarzan's Three Challenges, *1963.*

Jock Mahoney:
The Thirteenth Tarzan

FOR MANY YEARS, my wife and I followed a time-honored tradition in the Valley: sneaking the family into the Sportsman's Lodge pool for a swim. We'd park in the vast lot surrounding the Lodge at the corner of Coldwater Canyon and Ventura Boulevard, already in our swimsuits, and then saunter through the Patio Café entrance as though we were registered guests.

The Sportsman's Lodge is a hotel and restaurant and banquet facility that grew up around a man-made trout pond, where seventy years ago guests fished for their own dinner, to be cooked by the lodge's restaurant. Republic Studios was just down Ventura Boulevard, and many of its cowboy stars hung out at the Sportsman's Lodge, which was known at the time as the "Hollywood Trout Farms."

Legend has it that John Wayne taught his children to fish at the Lodge's ponds, which is something akin to teaching a kid to fish at the boathouse in New York's Central Park. If once a bubbling stream ran through the structure, what has remained is a meandering pool bridged by a wooden footbridge, ideal for wedding and bar-mitzvah photographs. Thousands have been taken there over the years. Swans, which have become the Lodge's trademark animal rather than trout, now glide along this little pond.

That is the banquet and meeting room end of the Sportsman's Lodge complex. The pool sits in a U-shaped gap of the adjoining two-story hotel. Balconies ring the swimming area, which has beach chairs and a Jacuzzi where I once encountered Jerry Stiller sitting in the bubbling water, reading a paper, a cigar in his mouth. This was the pool we requisitioned for our families, plopping our towels down on the deck chairs and nonchalantly wading into the water, projecting the aura of "guest."

In past years, that bit of nonchalant bravura wasn't really necessary. I'm sure most of the staff knew fully well who was a real guest and who was relying on the Sportsman Lodge's radical hospitality. Then there was a change in ownership, and the gates to the pool were locked, opened only by a room key. Visitors could purchase a day pass for ten dollars, be issued a wrist band, and gain entrance looking like someone attending an Eagles concert. The sweet juice of stolen fruit was gone. The new management also added a bar at one end of the pool, with loud canned music breaking what had been the serene peace of one of the best swimming pools in the Valley.

Until last year, when a remodeling began that is still in progress as I write, I would frequently walk in from the parking lot, passing through a tiled entrance next to the Patio Café. A series of plaques dedicated to those Republic movie cowboys lined the entrance: John Wayne, Gene Autry, Roy Rogers. And then there was a plaque with a name unfamiliar to most people today, but which I recognized: Jock Mahoney.

I recognized it because Jock's daughter, Princess O'Mahoney, was a fellow parent at our children's school. Her child had also been taught by Sebastian Cabot's daughter. The daughter of the English valet Mr. French teaching the granddaughter of "The Range Rider" of early television is a proper sort of Hollywood descendant decorum. You wouldn't really want the Range Rider to be teaching Mr. French, after all.

And yet, Sebastian Cabot the human being, if we may separate him from his best-known character, showed the streak of a surprisingly gruff revolutionary in 1967 when he recorded an album of poetry—reciting the lyrics of Bob Dylan. His rendition of "Like a Rolling Stone" is direct, forceful, in full American accent, perhaps the statement of a man who wished he was playing the Range Rider—freely riding the American Wild West, shooting it out with bad guys—instead of Mr. French, an indentured servant, playing the domestic role of pseudo-mother to a group of young children.

Princess is tall, strikingly good-looking, and athletic. Once I heard the story of her father, I understood that gene pool: Jock Mahoney was a handsome stuntman for years, then the star of Westerns, and at the age of forty-two became Hollywood's thirteenth Tarzan. He was the oldest man to ever play the role when, at forty-four, he appeared in his second *Tarzan* film. Jock Mahoney was a larger-than-life figure, a man whose physicality was completely intertwined with his work and his love of life.

His daughter, Princess, has been a successful and respected assistant director (AD) for many years. The AD position resembles nothing like what the title projects to civilians. The AD is not simply someone assisting the director. No, often it is the other way around, for an AD is the person responsible for the gargantuan task of scheduling every day of work on a film or TV show and ensuring that it all stays on schedule. It is the master sergeant of filmmaking. If the director can maintain a general's view of observing and directing the process, it is the AD who is on the ground, pushing the troops forward, mapping out each day's

Jock Mahoney with his daughter, Princess, on horseback.

conquest, battling the most implacable and relentless enemy known to man: time.

The first time Princess mentioned her father to me, she told his story in a kind of brief three-act pitch, typical of an AD's practiced habit of cutting to the chase:

> I remember when I was little, we had a big house. Then the work slowed down and we sold that house and moved to a smaller house. Then we moved to an even smaller house and I remember waking up one night because he had driven a Harley motorcycle right through the front door and onto our living room rug.

Like many loglines that reduce a hero's humanity to a footnote, Princess wanted to tell a fuller story, so we met at Art's Deli ("where every sandwich is a work of Art"), and I heard what it was like to grow up the daughter of a stuntman: "I was madly in love with him. Look—he named me Princess. I was the apple of his eye and I thought he was the most magnificent man."

Jock Mahoney was born Jacques O'Mahoney, of Irish, French, and Cherokee ancestry. He grew up in Davenport, Iowa, and attended the University of Iowa, where he was a champion diver. He enlisted in the Marine Corps in World War II and served as a pilot and flight instructor and then came out to Los Angeles after the war, like so many Midwesterners, and started doing stunt work: "He did high falls and horse work, he doubled Randolph Scott and Errol Flynn. He was an amazing athlete. That famous sword fight that Errol Flynn did, going up and down a staircase—that was all my father."

Princess leans across the table and whispers, as if her father might be in the next booth, "Between you and me, he was never a very good actor." It was Princess's mother who was the outstanding actor in the marriage.

Margaret Field was in *Wagon Train*, *The Virginians*, and *The Range Rider*, as well as the classic science fiction film *The Man from Planet X*. Jock and Margaret met while doing *The Range Rider*, which Jock starred in after he worked his way up the Columbia Pictures ladder. It was a ladder built on Westerns. Early on, Jock did stunts for Charles Starrett, who starred as the Durango Kid, a masked avenger in a series of Westerns. Because the character was masked, it was easy for Jock to do the stunts, and they became featured parts of the series.

In the late 1940s, Jock started to get small acting roles in a string of Columbia Westerns with titles that evoke childhood tales of the cowboy: *Roaring Rangers*, *Blazing Across the Pecos*, *Trail to Laredo*, *Horsemen of the Sierras*, *Renegades of the Sage*, *Lightning Gun*, *Texas Dynamo*. The string included the musical Western

Jock Mahoney with his wife, Margaret Field, in Acapulco.

Swing the Western Way, in which Jock portrayed Chief Iron Stomach, cheerfully offending Native Americans with a blissful ignorance.

The world of Columbia Westerns also embraced the studio's resident Three Stooges, and Jock appeared as the clumsy but heroic Arizona Kid with the Stooges in two-reelers such as *Out West, Square Heads of the Round Table,* and *Punchy Cowpunchers.* This uniquely American mash-up of slapstick vaudeville comedians with the Western genre was, in a strange way, groundbreaking. Consider Mel Brooks's *Blazing Saddles* and then the Billy Crystal film *City Slickers,* both funny because of the juxtaposition of Western icons with Borscht Belt comedians.

Then, in 1951, Gene Autry hired Jock to star in *The Range Rider.* His sidekick on the show was Dick Jones, a former child star who had provided the voice for Pinocchio. Such is the strange world of film; working with Moe, Larry, and Shemp one day, and with the voice of Pinocchio the next.

When Jock and Margaret Field met on the set of *The Range Rider,* she was a

L to R: X. Brands, Frances Bergen, and Jock Mahoney in a promotional photo for Yancy Derringer, *1959.*

divorcée with two children: a son, Richard, and the future Oscar-winning actress Sally Field. Margaret gave up her acting career to raise the children, and Jock Mahoney was living large. "He was so handsome and such a presence he could always command a room," Princess says. Jock was six feet, four inches tall, 220 pounds, and athletic, a "pretty good drinker, a smoker, and so good-looking he could get away with just about everything." They lived in Encino, where they had a one-acre backyard with horses, a pool, and a big oil barrel mounted on posts with a saddle strapped to it for practicing Cooper mounts, in which one leaps onto a horse from behind. Jock was famous for his ability to stand behind a horse fifteen hands tall, take one step, and leap onto the back of the horse without using his hands.

Jock had bows and arrows and guns. He shot a hole in the block wall behind the house, and he was always teaching Princess diving tricks, holding up the pool skimmer and getting her to backflip over it. He had a friend in the Valley who trained trapeze artists, utilizing an entire trapeze set up in his backyard, and Jock took

Princess over there for a couple of lessons. "It was a constant learning experience."

In those days, they had two Cadillac convertibles parked in the driveway, a red one and a white one. "He spent every penny he made. It was silly, but he enjoyed every minute." In the den of the house he suspended a Lionel Train track from the ceiling. The toy train went into a wall, came out from behind the bar, and circled back around. Every Easter morning, Princess would awake to find a string tied to her bed. She'd follow the string, winding through the big two-story home, like Theseus retracing his steps through the Labyrinth, to find her Easter basket. One year, her mother followed the string and it led her to a fur coat.

Jock bought Princess her first horse when she was seven:

It was a Christmas present. It was a beautiful little black horse. She had run away with a cart at Disneyland, and so they sold her and Dad bought her for me. I was told, "You always get back on a horse," so I spent most days with her bucking me off and me getting back on. Finally, he got rid of it. And then he wanted to get me a zebra. He had some friend who was ready to sell him a zebra, but I was too afraid.

Jock eventually purchased another horse, and Princess remembers riding it down Hayvenhurst Avenue to the Sepulveda Dam. This image boggles the imagination of today's residents, because now, as for as far as the eye can see, that area is saturated with houses, mini-malls, and apartment buildings.

Another man among Jock's menagerie of friends trained riders for the circus. He had a training setup in his backyard where people learned trick riding. (The Valley in those days was still half farmland, and backyards were more like the rear acres of an old farm.) A rope tied around the rider's waist led to a pivot pole in the center, so that if you fell off, you were hoisted back up into the air to wait for the horse to circle back around. Princess learned how to ride standing on a horse's back, how to turn around on a moving horse, and how to ride sitting backwards. Jock trained her in the entire diverse set of skills that make up the life of a stuntman, the bag of physical abilities that can be summoned for any job at any time. "It's completely different now," Princess says. "It's about driving cars and high-speed motorcycles, but back then it was high falls and swordfights and riding horses."

Jock and Margaret's best friends were actors Bill and Barbara Williams. Bill played the title role in *The Adventures of Kit Carson*, and Barbara was best known as Della Street on *Perry Mason*. Jock and Bill shared a boat in Newport Beach—the *Lively Lady*—and "got

Jock Mahoney riding bareback.

into a lot of trouble," Princess recalls. Jock and Margaret had big parties in the backyard all the time, enormous luaus, playing Martin Denny and his band on an immense RCA hi-fi. Denny, the "father of exotica," had been invited by Don the Beachcomber to play in Honolulu for two weeks in 1954, and effectively made the islands the home base for his band over ensuing decades. In his notes to *Incredibly Strange Music Volume 1*, Denny modestly described his musical style: "A lot of what I'm doing is just window dressing familiar tunes. I can take a tune like 'Flamingo' and give it a tropical feel, in my style."

Denny's celebration of Tiki culture was a perfect fit for the madness of Jock Mahoney's parties in Encino. Jock would decorate the backyard, don a grass skirt, a leafy headdress, and traditional Polynesian shin ornamentation, blast Denny and his band on the hi-fi, and launch into a spectacular Ote'a Tane dance, marching in pa'oti steps across the lawn: "Dad would have the whole outfit on, do the Tahitian dance, there would be little lights strung across the backyard, and Sally and I would make fun of him doing the whole thing. But he loved it."

Mahoney was intensely physical. He rode horses, he jumped from impossible heights, he fenced, he swam, he shot, he loved making craft projects with feathers and balsa wood—he lived for motion. The image of him in his heyday, in the Encino backyard, a horse in the stable behind him, a pool reflecting the little colored lights, Martin Denny and his band playing a crazy Polynesian dance tune on the hi-fi (the percussionist pounding on a Tahitian drum covered with a sharkskin, someone playing a nasal flute and another band member trumpeting a conch shell) while under the hazy Encino night sky Jock marches across the lawn, advancing like the traditional Tahitian dancer, mimicking a challenge to an enemy, exulting in his body and the freedom to move—this was the man born to play Tarzan.

And so he did. He donned the loincloth at an age when many Hollywood leading men begin a slow fade into character roles. It was a tribute to his physique, which remained like Adonis. The casting came after he appeared as the villainous Coy Banton in *Tarzan the Magnificent*. Producer Sy Weintraub, impressed with his work, decided the next time out, Jock should play Tarzan. Princess recalls:

> He was very proud to have done that role. It's a piece of film history. I still have a picture on my wall of him as Tarzan. Dad did two *Tarzan* films. They shot the first movie in India and the second one in Thailand. Mom went over to visit the set. There's a picture of Mom and Dad in India, riding an elephant. He told me that in one scene he was chained to a tree, with a tiger threatening him. He said they went and got a wild tiger and just let him roam around—it wasn't a trained tiger at all.

Weintraub's *Tarzan* films returned the character of Tarzan to the one Edgar Rice Burroughs portrayed in his books: an educated, articulate British gentleman who speaks in complete sentences, as opposed to the pidgin English "Me Tarzan, you Jane" we more familiarly think of as the character's essence. The Tarzan empire created by the book extended to the establishment of an entire suburb in the San Fernando Valley. Princess grew up in Encino, and just west of that neighborhood is Tarzana, where Edgar Rice Burroughs retired in glory. Ironically, it was to Tarzana that the Mahoney family would decamp within a few years. But at the moment, the first film was successful, and then came the shooting of Jock's second *Tarzan* feature, filmed in Thailand.

Princess remembers, "In Thailand, they asked him to jump out of a plane into the reservoir of a water treatment plant." A stuntman's life is made of a thousand small decisions that can mean life or death. The angle of a fall, the placement of a landing pad, the execution of a fencing move—dozens of things can go wrong with every stunt. None of Jock's family was there to witness Jock leaping from a moving airplane into a Thai reservoir. Today, it is inconceivable that a star would be asked to do such a thing. If nothing else, the insurance company would probably prohibit it. But that was another time, and this is what Jock did: high falls. He had built his life upon a spectacular physique and a willingness to take incredible chances. He was accustomed to leaping from great heights; he got his first break when no other stuntman would jump from an enormously tall staircase in *The Adventures of Don Juan*. And so he leapt from the plane into the reservoir.

One can imagine him standing over the open cargo door of a low-flying prop plane. There was the body of water—this was his job—and so he leapt: "The reservoir was actually a sewage treatment area and it was contaminated. He got infected with dengue fever, then dysentery and finally pneumonia. He lost a tremendous amount of weight—forty-five pounds—and never really recovered."

His body, that tremendous resource, the extraordinary athleticism upon which he had constructed his career and livelihood, was now wasted. Slowly but surely, his career declined:

We moved out of the big house to a smaller house in Tarzana. He built a huge waterfall coming down in the backyard. But he could never pay it off, and so we lost that house. Then we moved into a crackerbox on the border of Encino and Tarzana. My parents were breaking up. He was reduced to appearing in the TV show *Batman* as one of Catwoman's thugs. Then he got into a terrible movie with Raquel Welch. He was a motorcycle guy in that and one day he rode his Harley into our living room. I remember that motorcycle sitting in the living room of this little 900 square-foot house, the windows rattling, and he had these bug glasses on. Shortly after that, he and mom broke up. He went off with one of their friends.

By the end of Jock's marriage, his stepdaughter Sally had become a star in her own right as Gidget, Malibu surfer girl and iconic American figure. How did Jock handle that? Was he jealous? "No, he took credit for it. Sally took acting classes at Columbia Pictures and Dad always claimed he got her into those classes and got her started."

Sally Field continues to be a major star. She had a long relationship with Burt Reynolds. Reynolds loved Jock and crafted the film *Hooper* as a tribute to him and the world of stuntmen. Reynolds played Hollywood stuntman Sonny Hooper, and Sally Field played his girlfriend. Her character has a father named Jocko—a retired stuntman. This loving salute to Jock had an inevitable Hollywood twist: of course Jock wanted to play the role of himself, Jocko, but by 1978 he was not capable of handling it. Brian Keith did the part, and "it killed him, but that's the business. It's a business, no matter how you slice it."

He got work on a dude ranch in Colorado. They gave him a cabin there and he brought clientele in and showed them how to ride horses. He continued to work in film and television as long as he could:

> One day he was working on *Kung Fu*. He went to get on a horse, and he couldn't get on. He was having a stroke. He was staying with me at the time, and over the next ten years he had ten strokes. The tenth year he had an aortic bypass, and six months later he had a massive coronary.

Jock Mahoney passed away on December 14, 1989.

A stuntman's life is a double impersonation. Actors embody a character; stuntmen play the actor portraying the character. While doing stunt work, Jock Mahoney wasn't the Durango Kid; he was portraying the role of Charles Starrett acting the role of the Durango Kid. It is a peculiarly selfless sort of performance, in which the goal is to hope an audience believes you to be another actor. And the other actor will be doing an extraordinary feat for which his star will gain a luster and you will collect a thousand dollars and go home and soak your aches and wounds. Princess was emphatic when she said to me, "That famous Errol Flynn fight on the staircase—that was all my father. You can see it's him when you know it." She has the professional's pride in her father's work. Those on the inside know the limitations of what stars do—what portions the stars bring to the final film, and what portion is created for them by others.

Jock Mahoney had the unusual run of being both the stuntman portraying another actor's heroism, and then getting the chance to be an actor himself. He was an action star when action meant more than running while firing a handgun. The actions he performed were those of the backbone of American history: riding a horse, fighting with a sword, swimming a river. He was typecast, I suppose; the camera has a way of finding out the truth in someone, and Jock's truth was his love of physical action. He played that role to the end.

I no longer sneak into the Sportsman's Lodge. Like the Westerns of Columbia Pictures, those days are gone. Jock Mahoney's enormous backyard in Encino was subdivided into three lots, and there are suburban homes—safe and secure, with plastic swing sets in the backyards—where once there was a horse, and a barrel for Cooper mounts, and a man in a grass skirt dancing the Ote'a Tane under the San Fernando moon.

*Kathy Kohner (Gidget) with her father, Frederick Kohner.
Photograph by Allan Grant for* LIFE *magazine, 1930.*

Gidget,
Alive and Well in Malibu

FIRST OF ALL, Gidget is a real person. She is alive and well and she is Jewish. I met her on the deck of Duke's Restaurant in Malibu. She looked out at the Pacific Ocean, stretching deep and gray-blue to the horizon. From the shore, the water and waves look limitless. It is where one goes to become unmoored, adrift … free.

"People don't realize I'm real," she said. In the American mind, Gidget is Sandra Dee, she is Sally Field, she is the quintessential California girl of endless adolescence. But the real Gidget (short for "girl midget") is named Kathy Kohner Zuckerman, and she is the daughter of an émigré family from Bohemia whose father earned a PhD from the University of Vienna and then came to America from Nazi Germany in 1936. Bohemian Jewish intellectual Frederick Kohner wrote the novel *Gidget* in three weeks, and it set his life free and forever altered the course of his daughter's world.

Kathy Zuckerman works at Duke's a couple of times a week, greeting customers in the manner of retired champions like Joe Louis. If Joe Louis recalled for patrons the glory days of heavyweight boxing, Kathy is the living embodiment of an era when the joy of surfing played against a Beach Boys soundtrack and endless summer made Malibu a small town with an international reputation. She is seventy-two now, vibrant, with a beguiling smile, and carries herself with the fingertip-to-toe athleticism of a surfer. Her fictional doppelgänger is the celebrity; Kathy is an articulate woman who looks at her life with wry amusement but also a certain wariness. She was Gidget first, but the Gidget of the book and movies and TV show became an American icon and an industry onto itself. It is both her life and not her life.

Her father, Frederick Kohner, grew up in the same Czechoslovakian spa town that provided the setting for Ibsen's *Enemy of the People*. Frederick's father owned the local movie theater, and Frederick's older brother, Paul, managed to buttonhole silent film pioneer Carl Laemmle to interview him for the local newspaper when he was traveling in Bohemia. Paul had immense personal charm, and Laemmle attached him to his traveling party and ultimately offered him at job at his studio. Paul departed for America in 1921 and became an immensely successful agent in Hollywood. Frederick later wrote *The Magician of Sunset Boulevard*, a biography of his brother, chronicling Paul's lifelong friendship with and representation of people like Ingmar Bergman, John Huston, William Wyler, and Charles Bronson.

After earning his PhD, Frederick moved to Berlin to start writing screenplays. But in 1936, he joined the wave of Jewish intellectuals fleeing Nazi Germany, relocating to Hollywood when Paul got him a deal at Columbia Pictures. He wrote screenplays and two Broadway plays, and the family owned a house in Brentwood, but when I referred to Frederick Kohner as a very successful screenwriter, Kathy paused. She remembers 1954, when the family returned to Berlin because her father got a job with Arthur Browner writing for CCC Films. Presumably, there was no work for him in Hollywood at the time. But Kathy doesn't remember the family discussing money; it never seemed to be a problem, and in the summer of 1955, they came back to Los Angeles and their old ways, which included weekend excursions to Malibu.

Malibu is a tiny place that casts an outsized shadow. It runs along the shore of the Pacific Ocean for twenty-six miles and has a population of just over 13,000. The oldest tradition in Malibu—opposing development and walling itself off against outsiders—began with the founding family.

Frederick Rindge came west and purchased most of the land that is now Malibu. After he died, his widow Rhoda May Knight Rindge (known as May K. Rindge) began a long rearguard action against eminent domain, fighting the building of a railroad line through their property and then the construction of the Pacific Coast Highway. She went so far as to position hired armed guards at crossing points across her land. She even built her own small railroad on the property, taking advantage of a state law prohibiting railroad lines from running within two miles of each other. That strategy blocked the railroad (which to this day curves inland and skirts Malibu as it rolls along the coast), but in the end, after enormous legal fees, May Rindge lost her case against the Pacific Coast Highway and the dam was broken. She had fought for a certain sort of freedom—the right to say no to the government—and she lost.

The court costs and a declining economy pushed her into financial straits, and she started Malibu Potteries, an entrepreneurial attempt to regain her wealth. The company produced spectacular tile, which adorns almost every square inch of the walls and floors of the home she built for herself but never finished or lived in. (Now known as the Adamson House, it sits just north of the Malibu Pier, originally built to moor the Rindge yacht.) Trying to create a revenue stream from her property, May Rindge launched another enterprise, leasing homes to Hollywood stars in what became the Malibu Colony. The Colony quickly became a weekend destination for Hollywood's elite, but within a decade May's money woes deepened and she had to sell the land. The Malibu Colony evolved into exclusive homes for residents jealous of their privacy, and the Rindge heritage of keeping outsiders at arm's length deepened.

But if Malibu grew as a weekend retreat for the wealthy, it also grew in the obverse direction, as a home for vagabond surf bums. An oceanic phenomenon helped shape this other side of Malibu. In the ocean waves between the Malibu Pier and the elegantly tiled Adamson House, there are three breaks in the surf: First Point, Second Point, and Third Point. They are famous for holding the best surfing along this part of the Pacific, and surfers started congregating in Malibu from the time Duke Kahanamoku popularized riding the waves in the early twentieth century. These two strands of Malibu—Hollywood millionaires and surf bums—share a territorial instinct. The surfers stake out claims in the water, and newcomers must earn their way into the surf. And the millionaires wall themselves off from the public and hope that Malibu is a place where the world leaves them alone and free.

The Kohner family straddled the two worlds. Frederick and his wife loved the beach and socialized with screenwriter friends; Kathy loved the ocean and hung out with the surfers. The surfers—Matt and Buzzy, Moondoggie, the Cat and many more—congregated at the "shack," described in the novel as an "old Quonset hut made from bamboo sticks and palmettos and odd pieces of driftwood" where Moondoggie and other surfers lived during the summer.

Kathy bought a surfboard from fifteen-year-old Mike Doyle (later to become a famous surfer and shaper) and hit the water. She was fifteen and in love with surfing. She kept a diary that summer in which she recorded stories:

Kathy Kohner (Gidget) with surfboard. Photograph by E. Lenart.

… about my friends who lived in a shack on the beach, about the major crush I had on one of the surfers, about how I was teased, about how hard it was to catch a wave—to paddle the long board out—and how persistent I was at wanting to learn to surf and to be accepted by the "crew," as I often referred to the boys that summer.

I visited Kathy at her home, and she brought out three diaries from 1956, 1957, and 1958. They were small, thick volumes with green and red covers embossed with "My Dear Diary" and jovial 1950s illustrations of teenage girls. Each had a little lock, long since broken. They were filled with writing, and bookmarks were scattered between the pages. These records of Kathy's life during those summers are filled with romantic hopes and pinpoint moments in surfing history: the first day in 1956 when she tried surfing; records of "good combers" and "wiping out my scag."

Kathy can't remember whether she read aloud excerpts from her diaries to her father or he simply read them himself, but when she told him that she had an idea to write a story about her experiences surfing, Frederick suggested that he could do it for her. He talked with her, absorbed her bitchin' language, and three weeks later he had written *Gidget: The Little Girl with Big Ideas*. It was Frederick Kohner's first novel.

Kohner showed it to his brother, who passed on it. Frederick then took it to an agent at William Morris. The family was at the dinner table one night when Frederick got the call that all writers dream of—the magical, life-changing call that your ship has arrived. The William Morris agent told him, "Fritz, your book is going to be a movie. It's going to be a television show. It will set you up for the rest of your life." Fritz Kohner hung up the phone and never wrote another screenplay. *Gidget* came out in October, 1957, and Kathy remembers seeing it on the *Los Angeles Times* bestseller list at Number Eight—just in front of Number Nine, Jack Kerouac's *On The Road*.

Gidget is narrated by the book's title character, and Kohner captures the voice of a California teenage girl, a remarkable achievement for someone from a different generation, not to mention a foreign country:

> Boy, I sure felt right at home with the crew. They were regular guys—none of those fumbling high school jerks who tackle a girl like a football dummy. No sweaty hands and struggles on slippery leather seats of hot rods. The bums of Malibu knew how to talk to a girl, how to handle her, make her feel grown up. Every day—and I managed to come out to the cove almost every day—some-

one else let me have a board to practice ... [Surf]-riding is not playing Monopoly and the more I got the knack of it, the more I was crazy about it and the more I was crazy about it, the harder I worked at it.

Typically, an author writes about his own childhood, his fictive parents lurking in the background, often as antagonists. With *Gidget*, Kohner flipped this: he wrote of his daughter's childhood, and the fictional father in the background was himself. I can imagine him taking on writing the book as a sort of lark, with the predicted result being a light and sunny summer read. It became much more than that. Kohner irretrievably catapulted his daughter into the status of an American icon. He robbed her of her own autobiography, or rather captured it for her, in which case it no longer qualifies as autobiography, even though she is the title character.

The fictional Gidget as narrator takes in her world with unfiltered honesty. On page one, she swears she's about to tell us a true story, although she adds:

> On the other hand, a true story might not be a good story. That's what my English-comp teacher says—Mr. Glicksberg, that barfy-looking character who's practically invented halitosis. But then, he is dishing out a lot of bilge water if you ask me and what does a creep of an English teacher know about writing, anyhow?

Kohner's tongue-in-cheek irreverence toward his own background is threaded through the text. There is an oblique reference to Gidget's parents being naturalized, and her fictional father is a professor of German literature at USC. When Gidget tries to convince him to pitch in some money to buy her a surfboard, he is not happy, although Kohner uses the moment to reference the father/alter-Kohner's wide-ranging interests:

> Now my old man is a pigeon when it comes to promoting dough for a pair of skis, seats to the opera, the latest Fats Domino album, the Hungarian Relief, a new formal, a trip to Mammoth Mountain, but in matters "Moondoggie" I was biting on granite.

One senses Kohner enjoying taking on the voice of his daughter, poking fun at his intellectual life and the "zillions of books" he has around the house.

I asked Kathy about her parents' friendship with Lion Feuchtwanger, the novelist who escaped first Germany and then Nazi-occupied France and landed in

Sally Field as Gidget, 1965.

the Pacific Palisades. Feuchtwanger and his wife purchased the 6,000-square-foot "Los Angeles Times Demonstration Home," originally built as a model house of the future and intended to demonstrate the joys of living in a country/city environment. They picked it up for just $9,000, in part because it was viewed as too isolated from schools and hospitals. The Feuchtwangers dubbed their home "Villa Aurora," and it became a gathering point for the leading artists who fled Germany. Bertolt Brecht, Thomas Mann, and Arnold Schoenberg all socialized there, and Fritz Kohner was among them, although Kathy doesn't recall him bonding with those artists in particular.

Kohner seems to have shared novelist Thomas Mann's attitude about Los Angeles: "The climate has great advantages, as does the countryside, living expenses are relatively cheap, and in particular, the opportunities for our young musician-children are promising," Mann wrote to a friend. Contrast this with Brecht, whose poem, "Contemplating Hell," compares Hell to Los Angeles.

The world of émigrés and Brecht and Thomas Mann did not exist for Kathy when she was fifteen. That summer was all about going to "the Bu" and buying her first surfboard. That fall, the book was published and Kathy became a celebrity. She was now Gidget as well as Kathy. In her living room, as we spoke, she took out her high-school yearbook. Her classmates had signed it, addressing their notes to "Gidget" and often referring to her fame. But she wore her fame lightly; it was not a deep and abiding interest for her to be famous. She was a nonconformist, a tomboy. She was not a club girl or a shopper, but a surfer.

After high school, she attended Oregon State College for two years. Her father recommended she look up an excellent writer teaching there, Bernard Malamud. She never took a class from him, but instead became the Malamuds' babysitter for two years. She feels a character in his novel *A New Life* is based on her, although Malamud has denied it.

The movie version of *Gidget* opened while Kathy was in Corvallis, and she went to see it. She thought it was pleasant but divorced from the reality of her experience. Among other things, the actors playing the surfers were a far cry from the more rugged, tough Moondoggie. In real life, she was attracted to a surfer named Bill Jensen. Moondoggie was the handle for Billy Al Bengston, who became a well-known artist and still lives in Venice, California. Fritz Kohner liked the name "Moondoggie," so that became Gidget's love interest, even though Kathy never had a crush on Billy Bengston.

Kathy Zuckerman (Gidget) in her Pacific Palisades home with one of her diaries that inspired the book. Photograph by Ken LaZebnik, December 2013.

Her first boyfriend, perhaps not coincidentally, was from Hawaii. When he first saw her on campus, he said to a friend, "Oh, she's cute." The friend replied, "Forget it. That's that 'Gidget' girl." They dated, but Kathy missed Los Angeles. She came back home and tried the Peace Corps, but her nonconformist nature made that an awkward fit. The television show *Gidget* started its run, but Kathy could never relate to Sally Field.

Kathy Zuckerman, Gidget unchained, remembers she had no boundaries when she was a teenager. Her parents asked her to be home by midnight, and that was about it. She eventually married; her husband, Marvin, is a scholar and professor. Now married for nearly fifty years, she has grown children and grandchildren. One of her sons, Phil Zuckerman, is a noted author himself, often writing about religion from a sociological point of view, as in *Faith No More*.

The Gidget industry may have peaked in the 1960s, but it has never gone away. Kathy remembers traveling to Hawaii and seeing advertisements for Gidget products she never endorsed or even knew about. She taught in the Los Angeles school system for years—one year she had Cher as a student—and lived happily, but with a shadow always at her side. The fictional Gidget was never as bold as Kathy, never as free, never as thoughtful. The fictional Gidget was, of course, always a teenager.

Her father wrote additional *Gidget* books, taking the character on adventures to Europe and Hawaii. Some readers who knew that this was a father writing about his daughter in a roman-à-clef sort of manner speculated that a father's fiction of his daughter's coming of age—obsessed with boys and the size of her breasts—hearkened back to Kohner's Vienna days and called to mind a healthy dose of Freud. Kathy firmly rebuts those suggestions. "'Gidget' is a clean, well-lighted room. That's all it is." She must know there is a hint of irony in the reference, as the "clean, well-lighted place" of Hemingway's short story by that name is heavy with darkness.

There has been a documentary made of her life, *The Accidental Icon*, which underscores the essential existential dilemma of being celebrated as a fictional character. She is happy to promote Gidget, she enjoys making the sale when someone buys one of the books, but she is guarded about her life, too. She is selling Gidget, but she is more than Gidget and reveals that to the public at her own risk.

Now, at seventy-two, Kathy looks out at the Pacific Ocean. She tells me that her surfboard was blue and had a totem pole on it. In the TV series, Sally Field's board is bright yellow. (It is on display as part of John Mazza's Historical Surfboard

Collection in the "boardroom" of Pepperdine University's Payson Library.) A blue board probably wouldn't photograph well—it would get lost against a blue ocean, so the prop man got a yellow board. Does it matter? If your identity has been transmuted, reshaped by a thousand pecks, then the simple truths of your own life are a reminder that the doppelgänger spanning the world claiming to be you, a girl-midget named Gidget, is not authentic.

From the deck of Duke's Restaurant, Kathy gazes at the water and says, "There are no boundaries when you're out on a surfboard. You have a big page. Freedom. You're going down this wave—there's a kind of oneness with you and your body. No one else is controlling you in any way, shape or form." This is the light at the end of the pier in the world of Gidget. The waves of the Pacific curl in from across the world. They have come from Hawaii, and beyond that—the Marshall Islands, Polynesia, Borneo, the coasts of New Zealand. The Pacific dwarfs our concept of size; it is impossibly big, containing within it leviathans and a trash pile of plastic larger than Texas and the South China Sea and chains of islands and echoes of world wars and a girl midget riding on top of the ocean, carrying with her all of our dreams of freedom.

A Leigh Wiener GALLERY

THE HOLLYWOOD VAULT is an imposing Bauhaus structure set down among old warehouses and theaters on Seward Street. It is unmarked, save for a circular logo on the side of the building that looks like a canister of 35 mm film crossed with a Mercedes-Benz insignia. I drive up to a slatted aluminum door. A blue plastic fisheye security camera peers at me. As I reach for an intercom button, the aluminum door slides up at an incredible rate of speed, like a guillotine running in reverse.

I pull into a spotless garage with seven parking spaces. I could eat off the polished cement floor. In one corner is a little eating area, with an immaculate refrigerator, stove, and stainless-steel table. There is no eating upstairs in the actual vault, which remains pristine, a philosophy that apparently extends to the garage. At the far end of the garage is a glass wall, and visible behind it a stainless-steel elevator and staircase.

Above: Leigh Wiener beside his photographs of Charles Laughton and Grace Kelly.

The entrance to the Hollywood Vault, through this miniature and fantastical garage, transforms the utilitarian into the utopian.

Devik Wiener—warm, articulate, with the physical grace of a lifelong surfer—greets me. He is the son of the legendary photographer Leigh Wiener, who photographed movie stars, politicians, sports heroes, and American life from the 1950s until his untimely death in 1993. Devik spent eighteen months cataloguing 450,000 images shot by his father. They are all stored upstairs, secured within reflective steel vaults, along with cabinets of Crosby, Stills, Nash & Young masters, original demos from Barry Manilow, precious artwork, and film archives.

Devik pulls a plastic card out of his wallet, holds the card up to a keypad on the wall, and punches in a code. The entire corner of glass suddenly opens, two thick, transparent panes sliding back from a corner I had assumed was a permanent structure. It feels as if we are on the set of a *James Bond* movie and Q is about to issue us new equipment.

We take the stainless-steel elevator up a floor and enter into a sort of central bullpen. There's a viewing room, with clean, white surfaces on two sides. Flanking one side of the viewing room is a central control area, with seventeen monitors tracking various points of the vault. On the other side is a room ringed by glass. The entire Hollywood Vault is a dialectic between transparency and opaqueness.

Inside the glass room, sitting like a Claes Oldenburg sculpture, is an immense red cylinder of halon gas. In case of fire, the halon gas would suck the oxygen out of the air and extinguish the flames. All around me, the walls are spotless white above a textured stainless-steel wainscoting. One wall is dominated by a single slab of shiny steel. Running just below the ceiling of the room is a metal track that looks like something from a 1950s industrial assembly line. Mounted on the track at various points are cameras.

"Would you like a parka?" Devik asks. A row of metal hooks holds identical black parkas emblazoned with the Hollywood Vault logo. Devik hands me the kind of coat you wear in a Minnesota winter. "It's forty-five degrees in there." We don our gear and approach the slab of steel. Devik places an identity card over another security panel on the wall. A little light flashes and he punches in a key code. The slab slides open—it's a door on a track. Inside is a spotless hallway lined with high-density shelving units. The side of each polished steel cabinet sports a massive hand crank, clean and metallic, which looks capable of releasing a small reservoir.

Devik leads the way to the end of the long hallway. He spins one of the hand cranks and the high-density units roll back until they flank each other, opening up access to the one at the end. We walk into the revealed aisle. There is a shelving wall about twenty feet long and twelve feet high, every inch of which is loaded with archival boxes of Leigh Wiener photographs. Each box is labeled: "Judy Garland." "John F. Kennedy." "Frank Sinatra." "Sandy Koufax." "Robinson Jeffers." "Duke Ellington." "Paul Newman." "J. Paul Getty." "Groucho Marx." The boxes are a massive visual encyclopedia of twentieth-century American culture.

Leigh Wiener's father was a New York City newspaperman, and he often brought his friend Arthur Felig—better known as Weegee—over for dinner. Weegee brought photographs and laid them out for young Leigh's assessment, saying, "Remember, kid, tell me what you really think of them. My mother will tell me they're nice." Weegee answered all of Leigh's questions about the photos, their subjects, and how they were taken.

Leigh knew early on that photography would be his life's work. He sold his first photograph at age sixteen. His big break came in 1949. On April 8, a group of kids were playing in a field in San Marino, California, a suburb of Los Angeles, when three-and-a-half-year-old Kathy Fiscus fell down an abandoned well. The well was only fourteen inches wide and she was wedged ninety-seven feet down, crying for help. Within hours, hundreds of photographers, writers, and television crews descended upon the site. The world's attention became riveted to the plight of Kathy Fiscus. It became so huge a news story that for the first time in its history, *The London Times* held its edition, waiting to report the fate of Kathy Fiscus half a world away.

Leigh arrived at 8 p.m., hoping to take shots to sell to the Associated Press. Three hundred news reporters had been joined by a couple of thousand civilian spectators. Vendors were selling ice cream. It was a true media circus. Leigh walked away from all that, over a block to the Fiscus home. The kids Kathy had been playing with were sitting on the front step. Leigh struck up a conversation with them; making a human connection and understanding the psychology of a subject were always his primary tools. He took some shots of them and gave them the burned-out flashbulbs. Then one boy asked if Leigh would like to see the swing that he and Kathy often played on.

As Leigh tells the story in his book *How Do You Photograph People?*:

I followed Bus, Barbara, Stanley, and Jeeb to the rear yard. The swing hung from a tree. Near it were other tools of play—a wheeled hobbyhorse and an old tire casing. The scene was simple. No confusion. I put the camera on an orange crate and made six time exposures—varying in length from ten to thirty seconds. The older Lyon boy, Stanley, told me that he wanted to take pictures when he grew up.

Leigh turned the film over to an Associated Press courier and waited two more days until the rescue team reached the girl. By then, Kathy Fiscus was dead. Over 300 photographers snapped the shot of the lead rescuer emerging from the pipe bearing her body. But the shot used by more than 115 newspapers was Leigh's evocative photo of an empty swing. He captured the profoundly human emotion of the moment, something he did time and again over his entire career.

Leigh Wiener died far too young, at age sixty-two, of a rare blood disease. Doctors believe the disease was caused by exposure to nuclear radiation. In the late 1950s, while working for *LIFE* magazine, Wiener covered the atomic bomb testing near Las Vegas.

At the Hollywood Vault, Devik brings out an extraordinary box of photographs. On August 5, 1962, his father was assigned to cover the sudden death of Marilyn Monroe. He was the only photographer who got shots of Monroe in the Westwood Mortuary. He managed it with his usual combination of panache, guile, and artistry. He brought three bottles of Scotch to the morgue door, and when a security guard answered, he asked if Robert Ward was there. The guard didn't know a Robert Ward, which made sense because it was a name Leigh had made up. Leigh told the guard that he was meeting Ward there to have a drink—could he come in and wait? The guard let him in, and Leigh proceeded to open the Scotch and start pouring drinks for the little group of security guards. As Devik tells it, he got them talking about Monroe.

"I guess they have her down in Santa Monica," Leigh said.

"No," one of the guards replied. "She's right here." And he pointed to a wall of refrigerated doors. "You want to see her?"

"Sure."

One of the other guards hesitated, asking if Leigh had ever seen a dead body.

"I work for the Times. I've probably seen as many dead bodies as you have."

And so they took him to the refrigerated doors and pulled open the drawer that held the body of Marilyn Monroe. She was covered by a sheet. Leigh took pictures of the scene, of the guards, the drawer, of Marilyn's foot with a toe tag on it.

Then the guard asked if Leigh wanted him to pull off the sheet. "Sure," Leigh said. The guard pulled off the sheet. Marilyn lay in it, nude, autopsied. Leigh took some shots. Having captured this most valuable gold, Leigh departed. And he then did something completely in character: he decided he could not sell or show the photographs he had taken of Marilyn's body. It was too invasive; it would be disrespectful. He told reporters that he had placed those negatives in a safe deposit box, but Devik doubts that. "My father wasn't a safe-deposit box sort of guy. I think he just destroyed them."

Leigh also photographed Marilyn's funeral, which was tightly controlled by Joe DiMaggio, who refused to allow anyone from Marilyn's Hollywood world to attend. Leigh waited twenty-eight years before publishing the series of photographs in a limited-edition fine-press book, *Marilyn: A Hollywood Farewell*. Only 500 copies were printed, and the book has become a holy grail for Monroe fans.

Devik opened the archival box, and here were the original photographs from the book. The immediacy of large black-and-white photographs is visceral. But more commanding is Leigh Wiener's sense of the drama that comes from personality. He captured in the shots of the morgue guards a wonderful sense of their doughy personalities, which contrasted brilliantly with the glamorous body they were protecting.

In the late 1970s, Wiener created and produced a television series about photography, *Talk About Pictures*, in which he interviewed an assortment of photographers and photography lovers about the art. His co-host was his friend and photography enthusiast George Fenneman, best known as Groucho Marx's sidekick on *You Bet Your Life*. Leigh and George sat at a black table against a black backdrop, floating in space as they spoke to the likes of Ansel Adams, Alfred Eisenstaedt, and Lucien Clergue. More commercially oriented photographers stopped by, including *Playboy* photographer Mario Casilli; Henry Diltz, known for his rock album covers; and fashion photographer Milton Greene. Actors who loved shooting appeared, including John Astin, Ed Asner, Richard Chamberlain, Tippi Hedren, Roddy McDowall, and the now infamous Bob Crane, whose interests in photography were broad, to say the least. Other Hollywood figures were on the show, including director Sam Peckinpah, Lamont McLemore of the Fifth Dimension, and musician Graham Nash, who co-invented the high-resolution scanner.

Leigh himself was the subject of one broadcast in the series, and he told the story of how he captured a memorable image of the actress Simone Signoret at the 1959 Academy Awards. He starts with a typical Leigh Wiener bit of entrepreneurism: photographers were banned at the Pantages Theatre, so he bribed his way onto a temporary lighting platform with three bottles of Scotch. He continues the story:

> I had a 250-millimeter lens and a 35-millimeter camera. When you take pictures with a reflex camera, you never see the image, because the instant you expose it, the

Simone Signoret, 1960, the moment before she's announced as the Oscar winner for Best Actress in Room at the Top. *Pantages Theater, Los Angeles.*

mirror flips up and the image goes on the film. After the event, a courier picked up the film and took it to LIFE in New York. What I tried to get was the anticipation. If she had won the award, her expression would have been like everyone else's. People react very differently in anticipation. Almost all people react the same way in moments of triumph. That's easy. Watch how they react in preparation for triumph or loss. That's what I wanted from her. So I shot just before he said, "And the winner is…" At the word "is" I exposed it. This picture ran full page in LIFE. Three weeks after it ran, I got a letter from LIFE with a letter inside from Simone Signoret in Paris. She wrote "Dear Mr. Wiener, thank you for memorializing one of the most important moments of my life." She wound up the letter by saying, "In conclusion, Mr. Wiener, I think your photograph illustrates the old adage: 'In moments of crisis, we reach for those things we treasure the most.'"

Leigh Wiener photographed the faces of Hollywood in the moment—the moment of humanity, the moment of longing, the moment of performance—the moment that is, in short, the infinite present film gives us.

Ben Hecht, 1956

WHEN LEIGH WIENER went to Ben Hecht's office on the MGM lot in August of 1954 to photograph him, Hecht looked at the young photographer and growled, "How old are you, kid?" Before Wiener could tell him, Hecht asked another question: "Do you know anything about me?" Wiener replied, "I've read some of the stuff you've written and know that you've made a lot of money." Wiener later wrote, "With more a sense of satisfaction than bragging, Hecht replied with just a tinge of sadness, 'A helluva lot of money, kid, and I'd give it all back to be your age again.'"

Ben Hecht was a formidable figure, possibly the greatest of Hollywood's screenwriters, a man who could write a fine screenplay in two weeks and, according to his autobiography, never spent more than eight weeks on a script. The Writers Guild Foundation Shavelson-Webb Library has original manuscripts of some of Hecht's scripts; I have held in my hands the 154-page screenplay of *Notorious*.

Ben Hecht is associated with the freewheeling comedies that spun out of his Chicago newspaper career, starting with *The Front Page* and its descendants (including *His Girl Friday* and *Switching Channels*, starring Burt Reynolds and Kathleen Turner as television reporters). He wrote classic comedies such as *Twentieth Century* and *Nothing Sacred* and contributed to *Some Like It Hot*, but he also wrote the original *Scarface*, as well as *Wuthering Heights* (the version with Merle Oberon and Laurence Olivier), *A Farewell to Arms*, and the Hitchcock classics *Spellbound* and the previously mentioned *Notorious*. He is credited on more than sixty screenplays and carried no pretentiousness about the craft. He wrote in his autobiography:

> For many years I looked on movie writing as an amiable chore. It was a source of easy money and pleasant friendships. There was small responsibility. Your name as writer was buried in a flock of "credits." Your literary pride was never involved. What critics said about the movie you had written never bothered you. They were usually criticizing something you couldn't remember. Once when I was a guest on a radio quiz show called "Information Please," the plot of a movie I had written a year before and that was playing on Broadway then was recited to me in full. I was unable to identify it ... Hollywood held this double lure for me, tremendous sums of money for work that required no more effort than a game of pinochle.

Like those of the theater, Hollywood's so-called "death throes" have spanned generations. In his autobiography, Hecht deprecated film as "an eruption of trash that has

lamed the American mind and retarded Americans from becoming a cultured people." This is a bit of the *de rigueur* position on film that most American intellectuals took mid-twentieth-century; critiques of the studio film as worthy of commentary and admiration were another twenty years in the future. Now, with the dust of the studio props blowing somewhere over Africa by this time, we can consider the writer in Hollywood as more than the peripheral figure Hecht dismissed. He wrote of his books:

> The sad thing about writing fiction is that unless one writes classics one writes in a closet. Nothing can disappear like a book. The characters I made up are still alive … but in the closet always.

The characters of his novels are all shut away and forgotten. But the characters in his films get seen every day all over the world. It is the writer's plight to be remembered as the public wishes, not as the writer desired. All thirty-five of Hecht's novels are out of print; his films will never be.

Paul Newman, 1961

BORN IN OHIO, the son of a Jewish father and mother who practiced Christian Science, Paul Newman described himself as a Jew, saying, "It's more of a challenge." He was a leading man for decades. Film has a strange way of unearthing an actor's essence, and Newman's was that of a decent and generous man who was amazingly handsome but really would have preferred being known as a great actor rather than a movie star. Alas for him, he was a true movie star. He was both blessed and cursed with baby-blue eyes. He once joked, "I picture my epitaph: 'Here lies Paul Newman, who died a failure because his eyes turned brown.'"

After World War II, in which Newman served as an aircraft radio operator, he attended Kenyon College in Ohio, playing football and acting in plays. His father died in 1950, and Newman took over the family sporting goods store in Cleveland, only to leave after a year and a half and head east. He ended up with a role in *Picnic* on Broadway, where he first met Joanne Woodward. He was married at the time, and while the spark may have been lighted, nothing happened for several years. When they finally got together, their marriage lasted for more than fifty years, until Newman's death in 2008.

His first film was an infamous turkey: *The Silver Chalice*, in which he played Basil, a Greek slave who creates the cup used at the Last Supper. He took out an ad in *Variety* apologizing for his performance. Newman got his big break in 1955, taking over a lead television role James Dean had been scheduled to play before he died in a car crash. Newman appeared in an adaptation of Hemingway's short story "The Battler," which was part of a TV series called *Playwrights '56*. Arthur Penn directed the production, and it led to another role Dean was supposed to play, boxer Rocky Graziano in *Somebody Up There Likes Me*.

From that point on, it was off to the races. He took on two leading roles which were said to have first been offered to Elvis Presley but turned down by Colonel Parker: *Cat on a Hot Tin Roof* and *Sweet Bird of Youth*. One can only imagine Tennessee Williams's outrage (or hilarious delight) had the King essayed Brick or Chance. Then came a long string of commercial and artistic hits: *The Hustler, Hud, Harper, Cool Hand Luke, Butch Cassidy and the Sundance Kid, The Sting* … the list continued on for decades. He was charming, self-effacing, and devoted to his craft. He studied at the Actors Studio and felt that "I was always a character actor. I just looked like Little Red Riding Hood."

He was active politically, conducting an early fundraiser for Eugene McCarthy; he became a racecar driver, and then, late in life, a philanthropist. His Newman's Own brand has raised well over $300 million for charity. He once said:

> We are such spendthrifts with our lives. The trick of living is to slip on and off the planet with the least fuss you can muster. I'm not running for sainthood. I just happen to think that in life we need to be a little like the farmer, who puts back into the soil what he takes out.

On his seventy-fifth birthday, Newman held a ceremony on the front lawn of his Connecticut home and burned all of his tuxedos.

Jack Warner, 1963

THERE WERE four Warner brothers: Harry, the eldest, a serious moralist who believed that film could elevate humanity; Sam, who died young; Abe, remembered as easygoing and calm; and then there was Jack Warner. His son, Jack Warner Jr., wrote of his father:

> For years I have tried to find the keys to the labyrinth of my father's mind, but

it remains now what it was throughout most of his lifetime: boxes within boxes, rooms without doors, questions without answers, jokes without points, scenarios based on contradictions, omissions, and deceit. His was the anguished story of a man driven by fear, ambition, and the quest for absolute power and control—the little brother telling the big boys he saw as his tormentors to go to hell.

The Warner brothers' parents escaped the pogroms of Poland and settled in Youngstown, Ohio. In 1903, a nickelodeon opened in Pittsburgh, and Abe, Harry, and Sam all saw *The Great Train Robbery*. They knew in an instant that they should get into the movie business. The Warner brothers started their company on the East Coast in the early silent movie era, moved to California, and eventually became a major studio, known for their hard-hitting social issue signature films.

But within the industry, Harry and Jack became known for their murderous hatred of each other. Famously, Harry Warner once chased Jack through the streets of the Warner Bros. back lot, wielding a three-foot lead pipe and threatening to kill him. Jack outran his brother, who eventually hurled the lead pipe, missing his target. Producer and screenwriter Milton Sperling remembers the incident:

> Can you imagine? The president of Warners, a dignified old gentleman who had won hundreds of personal awards, chasing the head of studio production through the lot saying, "I'll kill you, you son-of-a-bitch!" It wasn't done in fun. It was deadly serious.

Jack Warner's daughter, Barbara, said of her father, "He was what you saw. You knew what to expect. He had a great smile, and great fun in life. He liked pretty women and good food." And his son, Jack Jr., remembered:

> I hear my father now in the executive dining room saying, "I'm not here to make friends—I'm here to run a studio and turn out movies to fill theater seats with behinds to make money for this company!" Perhaps Jack Warner wrote his own epitaph when he said: "I am what I am, and I will probably never change."

Groucho Marx, 1966

THE CONNECTIVE TISSUE between Leigh Wiener and Groucho Marx was George Fenneman. Fenneman was the sidekick for both of their late-career programs, serving as the announcer on Groucho's *You Bet Your Life* and alongside Wiener on *Talk About Pictures*.

You Bet Your Life began on radio in 1947 and finally ended its run as a hit television series in 1961. It showcased Groucho's improvisational comic riffs, and to capture those without offending the censors, each episode was recorded ahead of time, running about an hour in length, and was then cut down to half an hour. When the show shifted from radio to television, an unusual technique had to be adopted. So the flow of the program and Groucho's wit did not have to suffer stopping every ten minutes to change film reels, eight cameras ran, four pairs side-by-side, with a crew changing film reels in one camera to have it ready to start shooting from the same angle when the reel in its sister camera ran out.

Groucho's wit remains savagely funny long after his death in 1977. Some examples:

• After Groucho previewed *Samson and Delilah* starring Hedy Lamarr and Victor Mature, director Cecil B. DeMille asked him for his opinion. "It'll be a failure," Groucho said. DeMille asked, "Why? Why will it be a failure?" Groucho replied, "Because you got the characters wrong. Victor Mature has much bigger knockers than Hedy Lamarr."

• In Las Vegas, entertainer Ken Murray was speaking to Groucho after one of Murray's shows. Murray said, "I have trouble sleeping." Groucho shot back, "Have you ever tried sitting in your audience?"

• Groucho told the story of the time he went to see Houdini perform. At the time, Groucho was an unknown kid. Houdini did a famous trick in which he put needles in his mouth and a spool of thread, and then pulled out the needles, threaded. He asked for a volunteer from the audience to confirm there was nothing hidden in his mouth. Groucho walked up on stage and Houdini opened his mouth wide. "What do you see in there?" he asked. "Pyorrhea!" Groucho said, and left the stage.

• Once a priest approached Groucho and said, "I want to thank you for all the joy you've put into this world." Groucho shook his hand and said, "And I want to thank you for all the joy you've taken out of this world." The priest laughed—people always gleefully anticipated being insulted by Groucho—and asked if he could use that the following Sunday in his sermon. Groucho said, "Yes, but you'll have to pay the William Morris office ten percent."

Sid Caesar, 1962

IN 1949, *The Admiral Broadway Revue* was an immense hit, thanks mostly to its young comic star, Sid Caesar. It was such a big hit that the sponsor, the Admiral Television Company, cancelled it. Why? Because the show's blazing success had bumped the number of Admiral television sets being sold from 500 a week to 10,000. Rather than put their money into sponsoring a television show, Admiral

invested in producing more TV sets. Sid Caesar was instrumental in the last time manufacturing triumphed over marketing.

He grew up in Yonkers, where his émigré parents ran a twenty-four-hour luncheonette. Their clients came from all over the world, and as a child Sid Caesar learned to imitate the customers in a doublespeak that purported to be languages ranging from Italian to Russian to French to Spanish. The doublespeak routine became a staple of his comedy career.

Years later, after his towering success, he admitted in an autobiography that he was addicted to alcohol and barbiturates. He accepted responsibility for his addiction, didn't try to blame circumstance or anyone else, and the philosophy he emerged with at first read sounds like an example of doublespeak—except for its profound truth:

> There's a now, a was, and a gonna be. Now is now, and after now is a was. And what comes after the was is a gonna be. It hasn't happened yet. It's gonna happen as soon as the now is over. But if you have a good now, you're bound to have a good was and a good gonna be. But after the bad now comes a bad was. But if you have a bad now and dwell on it, you're going to have a bad gonna be and you're going to have a bad cycle. If you learn from the bad was, you can turn the bad gonna be into a good gonna be ... You need to learn from the wases. It's all about changing your attitude.

Al Jolson, 1948

HE WAS ONCE CALLED "The World's Greatest Entertainer," but today he may be the World's Greatest Forgotten Entertainer. Al Jolson was the Elvis Presley of his time. He co-opted black musical impulses, indeed co-opted blackface, brought it to white mainstream America, and became the biggest star in the world.

Jolson was born in Russia, the son of a rabbi, and in 1927 played the role that echoed his own life and changed Hollywood forever: Jakie Rabinowitz, who becomes a jazz singer going by the name of Jack Robin, in Warner Brothers' breakthrough film *The Jazz Singer*. Most people remember the famous line from that film, "Wait a minute, wait a minute, you ain't heard nothin' yet...," but don't realize the movie is about a young man from an Orthodox Jewish family whose desire

Al Jolson at Jeanette MacDonald's party, Hollywood, 1948.

to be a popular entertainer is in conflict with his parents' wishes. It is a quintessentially American tale—losing one's cultural heritage into the greater American stew. While it was about a Jewish family, there are parallels everywhere in American culture, particularly in the African American world.

Jolson had the star power to catalyze the talkie revolution. He was the biggest attraction on Broadway and in vaudeville. But if he is remembered by younger audiences at all today, it is for his blackface performances, which seem to brand him as a racial Neanderthal. Yet in the conflicted world of American race relations, Jolson was actually a fighter for racial equality.

As early as 1911, Jolson argued for the rights of African American performers. He promoted the first production with an all-black cast ever to be presented on Broadway (a play by black playwright Garland Anderson), and he demanded equal treatment for Cab Calloway when they performed together in the movie *The Singing Kid*. When he read that Eubie Blake and Noble Sissle were refused service at a restaurant, he took them out to dinner and they became good friends. As a performer, Jolson found the vitality and expressiveness of black music liberating, and many credit him with introducing jazz and blues to white audiences.

He was also an egomaniac. His second wife was the musical star Ruby Keeler, whom he met when she was a nineteen-year-old chorus dancer at Texas Guinan's speakeasy. He wooed her with extravagant gifts, including the promise of a million dollars, and they married in 1928. The next year Florenz Ziegfeld Jr. cast her in the starring role of the Broadway musical *Show Girl*. At the first preview, when she started dancing to the Gershwin hit song "Liza," Jolson stood up in the audience and began singing it. The audience went crazy, taking it as a sign of Jolson's support of his young wife, although it seems much more like a support of his own ego.

Leigh Wiener photographed a party for Jeanette MacDonald in Hollywood, and Jolson was in attendance. The year was 1948, and the star was past his prime, but the ego still burned hot. The original shot shows two musicians and Jolson ostensibly looking at a score. Except Jolson found the camera. Wiener recognized the glint in Jolson's eye, the unquenchable desire for attention, and closely cropped the photo to create the indelible portrait of an entertainer.

George Burns, undated

BORN NATHAN BIRNBAUM, the son of Jewish immigrants from Romania, George Burns became one of America's most beloved comedians and actors, with a career spanning the twentieth century, from vaudeville to radio, television to film. In 1932, he and his wife, Gracie Allen, launched their own radio show. It would live on radio and television over the next three decades. Burns was the straight man of the pair, and they perfected relationship comedy. The radio show developed into the prototypical TV sitcom, in which Burns and Allen portrayed themselves as performers with their own weekly program. Their supporting cast included music director Meredith Willson, acting the role of the naïve, girl-shy music director Meredith Willson. (He went on to write *The Music Man*.)

The television show pioneered a sort of Pirandello-metatext concept: at various points in an episode, Burns would turn on his TV, view what other characters were doing while he was offstage, and intervene in their story lines.

Gracie Allen, exhausted by the demands of weekly television, eventually retired in 1958. Burns continued a solo career that was unexpectedly lifted to new heights when he replaced his beloved friend Jack Benny (who was dying of cancer) in *The Sunshine Boys*. At eighty, he won the Oscar for Best Supporting Actor. He died at the age of one hundred.

Gregory Peck & Judy Garland, 1955

Gregory Peck with Judy Garland at the Hollywood Foreign Press Awards, February 1955.

LEIGH WIENER GALLERY

I HAD A PERSONAL BRUSH with the eccentric world of the Hollywood Foreign Press Association when I worked for Sundance. The HFPA supported Sundance Institute with a generous grant each year, and for many years they made a plea for Sundance founder Robert Redford to make an appearance on their broadcast. The President of the HFPA would call me up, ask whether I had heard from Redford—I had not—and then urge me to ask him again. To be clear, I wasn't the one making the ask; I would forward the request up the chain, and Redford would regularly decline, and the HFPA would search elsewhere for the stars that made their annual awards show, the Golden Globes, the moneymaker that helped bankroll their existence.

Within Hollywood, the HFPA show was for many years regarded as an amiable white-trash cousin of the Oscars; the awards were, after all, the decision of a few dozen newspaper correspondents representing places like Uruguay. The criteria for membership is that one publish four articles a year in a foreign publication, so the members are not so much the internationally respected European film critics as they are the entrepreneurial stringers who come to Hollywood and cobble together a career. Early on, they realized that by scheduling their awards ceremony before the Oscars, they could catch the rising wind of publicity and free studio junkets. One key to giving their ceremony a strong profile was getting celebrities to appear, so they served great food and lots of booze. The films nominated for HFPA Best Picture were often on the list only because their stars were considered most likely to show up at the Golden Globes.

The Leigh Wiener portrait of Gregory Peck and Judy Garland at the 1955 Golden Globes captures the dichotomy of the HFPA. From the waist up, here is Gregory Peck, elegant leading man, revered for his integrity even before it was stamped in the public consciousness as Atticus Finch. Peck made his mark as the star of *Gentleman's Agreement*, in the role of a newspaperman who goes undercover as a Jew to uncover anti-Semitism in postwar New York City. His agent urged him to turn down the part, feeling it would endanger his career. Instead, it earned him an Oscar nomination as Best Actor.

Just behind Judy Garland, we catch the outlines of Humphrey Bogart's face. He was a supporter of Garland and hated her husband at the time, Sid Luft, whom he accused of living off of Judy's talent. Garland and Luft lived at 144 South Mapleton Drive in Holmby Hills, in a home built by producer Hunt Stromberg. (It was Stromberg's son, Hunt Jr., who was monstrously cruel to Judy at the cancellation of her television show.) Their Holmby Hills neighbors were the typical assortment of stars one is always amazed to find living cheek by jowl. Two doors down from the Lufts, Humphrey Bogart and Lauren Bacall had a French colonial. Also on the block were writer Nunnally Johnson, as well as Art Linkletter, songwriters Sammy Cahn and Hoagy Carmichael, and Bing Crosby.

They all socialized at Bogie's home, although Bogart made matters uncomfortable for Luft. "Do you sing?" Bogart would challenge him. "No, you don't. Then why the hell are you making a living off a singer?" He would assert to Luft that class could never be bought and "I can tell you that you don't have it, my friend, and you never will."

Bogie admired Garland and gave her a pair of trick dice from *Casablanca* that always rolled eleven. In this photo, Judy Garland, in her 1950s pulchritude, was a gigantic Hollywood star, and was dressed for the role. But below the waist are the food, the cocktails, the cigarette, and the litter of the sensual pleasures of good living that lured even stars into the orbit of the Hollywood Foreign Press.

Darryl Zanuck, 1963

BORN IN WAHOO, NEBRASKA, Zanuck came to Los Angeles as an aspiring writer and spent the 1920s selling stories and scenarios to various producers and studios. He moved into the management side of Warner Brothers in 1929, became head of production by 1931, and in 1933 founded Twentieth Century Pictures, which became Twentieth Century-Fox Film Corporation in 1935 when it merged with William Fox's Fox Film Corporation. (Zanuck's wife, silent film actress Virginia Fox, was not related to William Fox.) Zanuck ran Twentieth Century-Fox on and off for nearly four decades.

Writer Walter Reisch, one of many Jewish émigrés from Vienna in the 1930s, was a stalwart writer of Zanuck's and loved the pace Zanuck set:

> Fox ... was like being in a big newspaper office. Everything went according to Zanuck's taste, Zanuck's speed, Zanuck's way of making pictures—that is, fast, topical, very little conversation, very few arguments ... When the day came that [Zanuck] needed you, you got an appointment via Esther, his secretary. She'd say, "Tuesday, 4 p.m., half an hour," and on Tuesday at four in the afternoon you got your half hour.

You walked in, and he told you exactly what you needed to know. There he sat with his cigar. He didn't even know your second name; addressed you only by your first name. He'd say, "I have to start a Clifton Webb picture on December 1st, and today is June 15th. I need the script within eight weeks because Webb has to read it, and as a perfectionist he takes a long time to learn his lines."

Among Zanuck's Oscars was one for producing *Gentleman's Agreement*. Zanuck decided to make the film after he was refused membership in the Los Angeles Country Club when they incorrectly assumed he was Jewish. Samuel Goldwyn asked him not to make the movie, fearing it would stir up trouble. It won the Academy Award for Best Picture of 1947.

John Wayne and Elizabeth Allen in a publicity shot for the film Donovan's Reef, *1963.*

Elizabeth Allen's
Garage Sale

A COUPLE OF YEARS AGO, I walked into a garage sale on Cantura Street and discovered I was in the home of a recently deceased actress of some note. In Los Angeles, garage sales frequently unearth the ephemera of show-business careers. Inside the front door of a Valley bungalow is a tomb housing the preserved detritus of an actor's forgotten life, with head shots serving as mummies and show souvenirs marking ancient sacrifices to the gods of entertainment; a Witt/Thomas coffee cup identifies that the deceased once made obeisance to the sitcom gods of the 1990s. Digging deeper into the table of old ashtrays, pencil sharpeners, and VHS tapes, one comes onto the next strata of shards, and there is a sweatshirt emblazoned with MTM, carbon-dating that relic to 1978.

The garage sale on Cantura Street took place in a broad one-story ranch house, with white clapboard on the outside and paneled wood on the inside. Framed photographs, posters from Broadway shows, theater books, and china dish sets were scattered around the living room. Standing off to one side was a large one-sheet picturing Paul Lynde sitting in a chair, flanked by two girls. Behind him stood a tall blonde man and a woman who was apparently supposed to be Lynde's wife. At the bottom was the logo for *The Paul Lynde Show*.

I had not been aware of this show and was staring at the poster when a woman wearing a spangly sweater came over, introduced herself as the estate-sale manager, and told me I was in the home of Elizabeth Allen. She looked at me for a moment and I pretended the name rang a bell. The woman said Allen was an actress and let it go at that.

Later, I did my research. Elizabeth Allen had been a leading lady on Broadway who started as a New York model and got her big break when she became the "Away We Go!" girl on *The Jackie Gleason Show* in the 1950s. Then she got serious about acting, appeared in several musicals, and ultimately was nominated for a Tony for her starring role in Richard Rodgers's short-lived *Do I Hear a Waltz?*

When that show closed early, she moved to Los Angeles and into the television industry, where she fell into the gray zone between "established star" and "working actress." She was a regular on *Bracken's World* and *CPO Sharkey* (a military comedy starring Don Rickles; she played his supervisor), and then came her television career high-water mark: the role of Paul Lynde's wife on *The Paul Lynde Show*. It is sweet to think of an era in America when audiences could accept Paul Lynde as a heterosexual husband.

The show was based on the play, *Howie*, about a lawyer whose eldest daughter marries a ne'er-do-well, then brings him home to live. The stage play was written by Phoebe Ephron, the screenwriter who often collaborated with her husband and mothered the four writing Ephron daughters. *Howie* had been produced in New York almost ten years earlier. In 1972, director and sitcom powerhouse Howard Asher saw it as a vehicle for a sitcom to replace his hit *Bewitched*. That show was ending its run in part because the star, Elizabeth Montgomery was divorcing her husband, the aforementioned Asher. He was committed contractually to ABC for one more season.

In its original conception, *Bewitched* explored issues created by a mixed marriage. In moving the "mixed" dynamic from black/white to mortal/witch, it illustrated one of network television's favorite illusions: one can replicate the issues of a societal conflict without the societal context that created it. The times they were a-changing, however, and ABC sought to have a comic response to the upheaval pictured in CBS's *All in the Family*. *The Paul Lynde Show* was to be that response—down to featuring the same fundamental setup of an adult slacker child returning to the family home. It hoped to deal with controversial current topics, but the network censors kept the clamps so securely on the scripts that it never achieved an edge.

With all those limitations, the show must still have been a monumental achievement for Elizabeth Allen. At the time, there were only three networks; to portray the wife of the star on one of those shows was enormous. The artifacts of her estate sale seemed to indicate its place in her pantheon. The one-sheet stood alone, showing Paul Lynde as the paterfamilias, and there was Elizabeth by his side, the wise and maternal wife providing stability to the wacky and ineffectual husband.

I wandered through the house on Cantura Street, past pieces of furniture tagged with pricing, searching for other clues to this life. Elizabeth's books were on the market, and as I looked through them I realized she had the same collection of Chekhov's plays, the same edition of Uta Hagen's *Respect for Acting* that I owned. It suddenly struck me

Elizabeth Allen and Paul Lynde in a promotional photo for The Paul Lynde Show, *1972.*

that everyone in the late twentieth-century theater had an identical shelf full of aging paperback copies of *Dance to the Piper* and *Acting Is Believing*, and that garage sales in regional theater cities across America would display the identical books. It was as if we had all attended the same theater Tupperware parties over the past decades.

The sales manager was also selling Elizabeth's old head shots, for ten dollars each. That seemed like a lot for an old head shot of someone I neither knew nor remembered as an actress, but I bought one because I felt some strange kinship to her. Perhaps she was important and I failed to recognize it. Perhaps I am important and no one has managed to recognize me.

Looking through the head shots, I struck up a conversation with another browser at the estate sale. This was an older Italian woman who confided to me, "I am Sergio Franchi's sister. They had a big romance." Sergio Franchi was a name I did recognize. He was the popular Italian singer, a favorite of Las Vegas and *The Ed Sullivan Show*, and the older Italian woman whispered to me that he had been Elizabeth's costar in *Do I Hear a Waltz?* "During the show—a very big romance. Very intense."

Sure enough, there were photos on sale of Elizabeth and Sergio in the production, shots now over forty years old, commemorating a secret romance played out on stage. I examined a color photo of Sergio and Elizabeth from *Do I Hear a Waltz?* It had deteriorated over time; the color process had seeped detail from the shot, and the stage background bled amber. Sergio and Elizabeth were singing to each other, wearing costumes redolent of the late 1960s, and I was struck by the ghostly image of a lost illusion. Both are now gone. Sergio's sister was obviously in on their romance, and I wondered how often she had been in this house. Had she befriended her brother's amour, and was she there as a representative of a lost love, collecting a personal momento or two to preserve the memory of her brother's passion? Or had she turned up precisely to gather some information she was never privy to? Either way, we were both scavengers of history. And, I noted, she passed on purchasing the old *Do I Hear a Waltz?* poster.

It has never been clear to me which sister of Sergio Franchi I stumbled upon. I like to believe it was his younger sister, Dana Catalano, who had a performing career of her own and then became a spiritual healer, drawing upon her musical background to discover (her website tells us) a "correlation between the vibrations of the twelve Zodiac signs and the twelve notes in our Western musical scale. This insight founded the music theory embodied in [my] zodiac vibrations music library."

Like many an archaeological dig, Elizabeth Allen's garage sale contained artifacts from adjoining civilizations and eras. No tomb is an island; she ventured out into the world, gathered material items, and returned; she was visited by foreign dignitaries, who in turn left their mark. Thus *The Paul Lynde Show* poster has invisible roots in the life of William Asher, who cut his teeth as a director for *I Love Lucy*. Asher was traditional Hollywood's attempt to pivot into relevance in the 1970s with *The Paul Lynde Show*. To the studio mind, Asher made sense;

Sergio Franchi in a publicity shot for The Secret of Santa Vittoria, *1969.*

after all, this was the man who directed the string of 1960s beach movies with Frankie Avalon and Annette Funicello—*Beach Party, Muscle Beach Party, Beach Blanket Bingo,* and (with Dwayne Hickman subbing for Frankie) *How to Stuff a Wild Bikini.* They were low-budget hits with teenagers, even as they included cameos from Hollywood's past: Buster Keaton, Boris Karloff, Mickey Rooney. *Muscle Beach Party* also included the screen debut of Stevie Wonder. Elizabeth Allen and William Asher were perfect bookends, framing the 1950s world of Sergio Franchi and Hollywood on one side and the day-glo 1970s on the other.

And what of Elizabeth Allen's fate? Show business has a particularly intense relationship with memory. The tributes the Academy Award broadcast contains each year to those who have passed away; the tributes almost every award show carries to the living dead, honoring some ancient actor who totters onstage to a standing ovation and a mildly surprised reaction of millions of Americans watching at home ("I didn't know he was still alive!")—those tributes underscore the associations the public carries with the images of films as landmarks within their own lives. Thus, when I see a clip of *Annie Hall,* it takes me back to my youth and a time when I thought Diane Keaton epitomized everything alluring in a woman. When my mother-in-law sees an old Errol Flynn movie on television, it conjures the romantic image she had of him in 1950 and that time in her own life.

As I read of Elizabeth Allen's death at seventy-seven, I walk through the online garage sale of her life on Google images: past the head shots of when she was New-York-City-model beautiful; past her time as Jackie Gleason's "Away We Go!" girl and her appearance on *Twilight Zone*; then the shots of her and John Wayne from *Donovan's Reef*; and then suddenly her hair is strangely puffy and she is posing with Paul Lynde, looking matronly where she never had before; then there she is with Leslie Neilsen in *Bracken's World,* thank God the puffy hair is gone and she looks sophisticated again; then there is a copy of the *42nd Street* program; and then there is the obituary.

Thankfully, Elizabeth's obit runs with a photograph of her and Sergio from *Do I Hear a Waltz?,* framed forever as a couple. She is gone, her possessions dispersed. Her house on Cantura Street was sold and torn down, and a McMansion stands in place of her low-slung ranch house. We will all be faint memories one day. The Jewish tradition states that as long as one is remembered, one is not truly dead. But for all but a handful of individuals through human history, that is not the case. We are in the world and then we are gone, because there is something more authentic than memory, which we call the here and now.

Dick Powell publicity shot, 1938.

The Dick Powell Show
Grades Jack Nicholson: C+

SILHOUETTES OF LIGHTING EQUIPMENT, cameras, and a boom mike appear across the immense back wall of a soundstage. Enormous double doors, two stories high, slowly swing open. A shaft of light falls through. A man walks into the light. A title card appears on the screen: THE DICK POWELL SHOW.

Dick Powell strides down the alley of light toward a cluster of director chairs, boom microphones, spotlights on high stands, and a lighting control panel with big pull levers. He turns a corner and moves through an array of pedestal cameras, cables, and lighting gear. He speaks right to the camera, addressing us all at home, curled up on our couches in 1961, ready to hear him tell us a story.

Fifty years after Powell's death, his son Norman Powell leafs through a script from *The Dick Powell Show* in the archives of Pepperdine University Libraries. Norman, the fittest 77-year-old one will ever meet, turns to a production unit credit page, and there is his name, as unit production manager. *The Dick Powell Show* was a hinge between the early days of intelligent black-and-white television drama and its ripening into color and banality, and Norman remembers it all.

The Dick Powell Show was one of the last gasps of a great television tradition for writers, the dramatic anthology series. When TV began, the infant medium was a live event, and since much of the production was centered in New York, one might assume the Broadway theater was a natural source of material for one-off productions. As is often the case with television, however, beyond the acting talent pool that Broadway offered, radio provided the real antecedent. Radio series such as *The Jack Benny Program* and *Gunsmoke* became the first staples of television, but in addition to material, television also imported a structural mechanism from radio: the predominance of the writer.

In film, the studios made producers the dominant force, and then directors took sway. But in radio, with its need for vast amounts of material, the writer/producer

Dick and Norman Powell, undated.

became the auteur. That tradition carries through to television programming today.

The script Norman holds once belonged to Stanley Kallis, associate producer for the show, and is part of the Stanley M. Kallis collection at Pepperdine. The cover sheet is a tan card stock, emblazoned with *The Dick Powell Show* logo, balanced at the bottom with the Four Star logo. Typed in the top right corner is the episode's title, "John J. Diggs." Sprinkled across the cover are Kallis's penciled notes: "Gonzales stunt double topples down stairs SC 14." "Valdez has car." "Extras: Mexican policemen—clean cut—personable."

Inside is a pink sheet, indicating a revision, with the budget detail for the art department, including the cost of signs for EXT. MEXICALI STREET (Location Venice): AMOUNT $1125. "Bozo's Café" is also in Venice for exteriors, but the

INT. BOZO'S CAFÉ will be shot on STF 4 at a cost of $850. A credits page tells us: "Original Teleplay Written Especially for *The Dick Powell Show* by Albert Beich and William H. Wright. Producer Ralph Nelson, Executive Producer Dick Powell, Director Ralph Nelson. Revised June 1, 1961."

The script itself is a tough-minded piece about an American, John J. Diggs, played by Dick Powell, who works along the border. He's a guy with a checkered past—he's been in and out of jail—but a high-minded streak emerges as he protects the son who doesn't know Diggs is his father. At the beginning of the piece, Diggs has just gambled away his last $100 in a Mexican craps game:

GOLD TOOTH: How much you lose, Diggs?

DIGGS: Three months in the hot sun.

GOLD TOOTH: (laughs) You come to my house, I give you tacos.

Diggs gets a job repainting stolen cars, then crosses the border and starts working for a widow running a hotel and bar. She's got an attractive seventeen-year-old daughter, but it's the widow he makes a play for by the end of the piece. The script is constructed tightly, written in a terse style, a sort of *Treasure of the Sierra Madre* crossed with *A Touch of Evil*:

He gets his hat.

MARGO: Wait—you look like you're down on your luck.

DIGGS: Not me—I'm a secret agent for the FBI. We all dress this way.
He starts for the door. She opens her purse.

MARGO: Here.

He turns—she hands him a dollar bill.

DIGGS: What's that for?

MARGO: (smiles) Even an agent should shave once in a while.

DIGGS: (thoughtfully) Say—you wouldn't have about ninety-nine more of those lying around, would you?

MARGO: Well, of all the ungrateful—

DIGGS: It's part of life, Ma'am. Someone gives you a hundred dollars, it's a loan. You take a buck—and you're a bum.

MARGO: (looks him over carefully) And you're no bum.

DIGGS: (grins) No, ma'am.

Goes to door, looks back at her.

DIGGS: (continues; still grinning) Not yet.

There is a small role for a young punk named Eddie. He's in a stolen-car racket and corrupts Diggs's son Jack. On the back of the script are penciled notes by Kallis, who graded the actors auditioning for various roles. Five actors read for Jack. Michael Parks got the role, and he continues to work today, appearing in *Django Unchained* and *Argo* just this year. Three actors read for the role of Eddie. Dee Pollack got a B, Chris Robinson got a B–, and Jack Nicholson got a C+. The role went to Anthony Call, who came in to read for another part and ended up with the role of Eddie. Jack Nicholson went on to other things.

The script contains an ending in which John J. Diggs is shot, convinces his son to turn himself into the police for stealing a car, and then either dies as the police take away his son, or hangs on long enough for the widow to join him in a toast. One can almost hear the network note that might have dictated this alternate dramaturgy: "We feel to allow Diggs a final toast with the widow could redeem him and make him more likeable. It lets the episode end on a victory rather than the hollow feeling of dying as his son is going off to jail."

Dramatic anthologies on television provided some of its earliest hit shows, such as *Fireside Theatre*, *The Philco Television Playhouse*, and *General Electric Theater*. This came to be considered the Golden Age of TV, although many would argue the past decade of cable TV has produced a more mature and deeper golden age. By 1960, television had settled into a fondness for continuing series. There was more money to be made by having a familiar star that people would tune in to each week, rather than relying on the ups and downs of introducing a new piece, a new world, a new cast of characters each week and hoping that an audience would continue to tune in. *The Dick Powell Show* was one of the last to buck the trend,

Jack Nicholson in The Little Shop of Horrors, *1960.*

and like most things Dick Powell did in his life, it was successful.

Powell started his career as a handsome, boyish crooner with big bands, and moved to acting in films. His improbable casting as Lysander in Max Reinhardt's film of *A Midsummer Night's Dream* was a mistake he was aware of, and he tried to get out of doing the role. He couldn't, and the film's wildly uneven performances—ranging from Mickey Rooney's hyperventilating Puck to little person Billy Barty playing Mustard-Seed—doomed the entire enterprise.

(In the 1990s, I went to a pharmacy in Toluca Lake. The far end of the counter had been cut down to about three feet high and was labeled "Billy Barty's Prescription Counter." I had my own encounter with the irrepressible Barty on the short-lived dramedy *Jack's Place*. An episode I wrote featured a leprechaun and ultimately a black doo-wop group singing "Danny Boy." Barty was the leprechaun. He quickly identified me as the writer of the episode, and even though this was my first job, immediately pitched several story ideas involving the continuing drama of the leprechaun. No wonder the man worked his entire life.)

Returning to Dick Powell: Norman remembers a childhood summer that provided the pivot to Powell's career. Dick Powell's success as a crooner had resulted in a home in Hollywood and a vacation place in Newport Beach. He was married to actress Joan

Blondell, who had grown up in vaudeville (her father was one of the original Katzenjammer Kids) and made her mark in films as diverse as *The Public Enemy* with James Cagney and *Gold Diggers of 1933*, in which she costarred with Ruby Keeler and future husband Dick Powell. Typically, Norman and Joan Blondell would spend time in Newport Beach while his father toured. But that year was different. In Norman's words, "Up until that summer, Dad was working all the time. Then he was home all summer. He was out of work for three months. He knew he had to do something. He had to remake himself."

Powell lobbied hard for the lead role in *Double Indemnity* but lost out to Fred MacMurray. He persisted in pursuing a tough-guy image, and finally director Edward Dmytryk cast him as Philip Marlowe in *Murder, My Sweet*. It was a hit, and Powell went on to play leads in films like *Johnny O'Clock* and *Cry Danger*. He was *Richard Diamond, Private Detective* on NBC radio for four years in the early 1950s, with many episodes written by the young Blake Edwards.

Was Dick Powell a tough guy like the ones he portrayed on screen? Norman replies:

No. He was intellectually courageous, but he was not a tough guy in the sense of picking a fight. He was a very decent guy. Ronald Reagan was asked to describe him and replied, "What you see is what you get. He's a straight shooter." I didn't know anyone who didn't like Dad.

Beyond acting, Powell was interested in producing and directing. He taught himself to direct and secured a movie deal and office at Fox. With the help of Abe Lastfogel, his William Morris agent, he put together a business plan for a production company called Four Star productions. Four stars would head it: Powell, Charles Boyer, David Niven, and eventually Ida Lupino.

Powell came up with an idea for an anthology series. *Four Star Playhouse* would feature the four stars taking turns as guest hosts, week to week. The show premiered in 1952 with Powell, Boyer, and Niven. The fourth star was initially a guest slot, and then Lupino stepped into that role. For its first season, *Four Star Playhouse* ran only on alternate weeks, sharing a time slot with the television version of *Amos 'n' Andy*. But for the next three years it ran weekly and was on the air until 1956.

Immediately following the end of *Four Star Playhouse*, Powell launched another anthology: *Zane Grey Theatre*, which was in large part responsible for the run of Westerns on television in the 1950s. It hosted the pilot episodes of *The Westerner* with Brian Keith and *The Rifleman* with Chuck Connors. The first episode of *The

Rifleman was written by Sam Peckinpah, who was one of many creative forces Dick Powell helped nurture. Steve McQueen, Mary Tyler Moore, Linda Evans, the Smothers Brothers, and Lee Majors all got their start under the Four Star banner, and Powell gained a reputation as a leader sympathetic to his creative staff.

Norman Powell became friends with Steve McQueen on the set of the Four Star production *Wanted: Dead or Alive*. McQueen would ride his Triumph Bonneville motorcycle into the studio, roaring in on his rear wheel only. Dick Powell, understandably concerned about a potential accident sinking his new star and show, wrote into McQueen's contract for the second season that he was prohibited from riding motorcycles. Norman was unaware of this when McQueen offered to sell him the Bonneville. He remembers, "I bought the bike. My dad, always appreciative of ingenuity, graciously took us to lunch where they both admonished me to ride carefully."

Then, in 1961, *The Dick Powell Show* premiered. Throughout the 1950s, television had been undermining movies, and now the studio system was collapsing. *The Dick Powell Show* represented a sort of bridge between old Hollywood, with its geographic center in movies, and the more profitable new Hollywood of television. Many film stars were happy to do an episode of television, which played into the nature of an anthology program. Robert Ryan, Robert Mitchum, Mickey Rooney, Tuesday Weld, and Dana Andrews were just a few of *The Dick Powell Show*'s guest stars.

The series was also a launching pad for many writers and directors, including Aaron Spelling, Peckinpah, and William Friedkin. It debuted the pilot for what became *Burke's Law*—a script entitled "Who Killed Julie Greer?" starring Powell as Amos Burke and featuring Ronald Reagan as the killer.

Norman remembers one notorious incident that resulted from the influx of film stars into the television world. Rosemary Clooney and Lee Marvin starred in "The Losers," written by Bruce Geller, who went on to create *Mission: Impossible*, and directed by Peckinpah. This script is also in the Stanley Kallis collection, and I leafed through its pages of daily production reports, the forms all neatly filled out by hand: "Lee Marvin—Make Up 8A, Time Called 8:30A, Time Dismissed 7P." Also in the cast was Marvin's old drinking buddy, Keenan Wynn. This note appears on the production report for Tuesday, October 2, 1962: "Wrapped at 7:05, due to Keenan Wynn unable to continue."

Perhaps that was the day of the incident. Norman recalls that following a long night of barhopping, Marvin and Wynn showed up on the set still drunk. He remembers what happened next:

Lee Marvin in a publicity shot for The Twilight Zone *episode "The Grave," 1961.*

Lee groped Rosemary really badly. I mean, it was really bad. Terrible. She filed a complaint with SAG. At that time the decision about disciplining actors was left up to the producer. My dad called me into his office when he had Lee Marvin come in. Lee appeared and he was deeply apologetic. He was sorry, he felt awful, it was the liquor. My father looked at him, accepted the apology, and let him go. After Lee left, he turned to me and said, "How could I do something to him? He's three times the actor I'll ever be."

Thus ever with movie stars. Inexcusable behavior is excused, which may say as much about human nature as it does the culture of celebrity. The urge to deify is as strong as the urge to scapegoat.

In 1956, Powell directed the feature film *The Conqueror*, starring John Wayne as Genghis Khan in one of Hollywood's most outrageous pieces of miscasting. It should be noted that wasn't Powell's idea. John Wayne was discussing scripts in Powell's office one day, and when Powell had to leave momentarily, Wayne picked up a copy of *The*

Conqueror, which Powell had intended to throw away. Wayne started reading and fell in love with it. When Powell returned, Wayne was adamant that he wanted to play the role. Dick Powell famously said, "Who am I to turn down John Wayne?"

The Conqueror has become a legendary film disaster, both as a piece of art and as a tragic encounter with radiation. It was shot in St. George, Utah, just over 100 miles from an aboveground nuclear weapons testing site. Government officials assured Powell and producer Howard Hughes that the location was safe, but within fifteen years of the filming, ninety-one members of the 220-person cast and crew were diagnosed with some sort of cancer.

In the end, the death toll included leads John Wayne, Pedro Armendáriz, Susan Hayward, Agnes Moorehead, and Dick Powell himself. Reportedly, Howard Hughes so regretted the project (which wags dubbed "An RKO Radioactive Picture") that he bought every copy of the film for $12 million and had them all locked away in his Las Vegas apartment, where he obsessively viewed the film as his fingernails endlessly grew. Norman Powell remembers the shoot well:

> We shot the film in St. George, Utah, and the set was a bed of debauchery. I was a kid of 21, I was hanging out with Patrick Wayne, John's son. We both played Mongol guards. I had one line: "Halt, who goes there?" We were out in the middle of the desert and everyone was drinking and screwing around. I remember walking by one actress's trailer and she reaches out and hauls me in and I had to fight my way out of there ... The saddest part was that we filmed there and then had to do pick-up shots back in Los Angeles. They couldn't find the right kind of dirt to match the dirt from St. George, so they trucked in loads of this radioactive dirt to Hollywood.

Norman still has a Four Star ashtray in his home office: "Dad died of cancer, as did all those other folks from *The Conqueror*, but he also smoked heavily. Everyone did back then." *The Dick Powell Show* lasted after Dick's death, with guest hosts taking on the introductory duties. But Four Star was thought of as a one-man shop. The company had gone public before Dick Powell died, but once he was gone, the stock collapsed.

The final episode of *The Dick Powell Show* aired on April 30, 1963. It was hosted by Ronald Reagan and starred Bob Cummings. The title: "Last of the Private Eyes." In a fitting tribute to Dick Powell's legacy as a hard-boiled detective who never seemed like a tough guy to his friends and family, Cummings plays a former movie usher who wants to be a private eye. He ends up discovering that life is just like the movies.

Mel Shavelson, undated publicity shot.

Mel Shavelson
and the Last Bugler

ONE SATURDAY MORNING, I walked up Laurel Canyon to Sunshine Terrace and another Los Angeles garage sale. The house was large, the lot extensive, including a tennis court; clearly this had been the home of someone successful. The aesthetic feel was of prosperous Los Angeles suburban life circa the mid-1970s: a ranch house, but expansive, set on a lot that could accommodate at least two homes. A big picture window opened to the backyard, and the walls were wood-paneled around a sunken living room. There was a study with large bookcases and some framed photographs, and binders filled with writing. I picked up a binder and opened it to the first page: "Melville Shavelson: THE LITTLE BUGLER."

I was in the home of a former president of the Writers Guild of America, West (WGAW), an enormously successful Hollywood writer—and, outside the industry in 2013, a man probably unknown. Mel Shavelson was important. Or was he?

I purchased a framed photo of Mel, and the binder, which was filled with two-and-a-half inches of the scenario, notes, and first pages of *The Little Bugler*. The photo now hangs in my office, and I'm sure some take it as an ironic gesture: a black-and-white head shot of a smiling bald man in a dark suit, holding a pipe as the sort of prop that was intended to signify "intellectual." His photo is not ironic to me; he was one of Hollywood's most successful writers, voted a leader of his peers, and a studious craftsman, which I can verify from the binder. And yet ... and yet ... would Hemingway ever have posed for this photo, which could just as easily have been a portrait of a successful Madison Avenue executive? What grime of commerce distends that grin in the picture, a smile that seems intended to assure the viewer, "I'm easy to work with. Nothing to fear here"?

To begin with, it must be noted that Shavelson was a comedy writer. He was born in Brooklyn in 1917 and named Melville Shavelson because his mother loved *Moby-Dick*. As he writes in his autobiography: "[I was born] above the toy store my father owned at 1010 Flatbush Avenue, Brooklyn, New York, an address I left as soon as I found out where I was." That tone permeates his autobiography. He can't resist a joke, which creates a wall of sorts around difficult experiences.

Shavelson attended Cornell University, and after graduation started in radio. He got his big break writing for Bob Hope. His autobiography, *How To Succeed In Hollywood Without Really Trying P.S.—You Can't!*, was published after Hope's death and allowed him to include such interesting tidbits as the way Hope distributed paychecks to his writers. He folded them into paper airplanes and sailed them across the room so they'd have to run and catch them.

It was on Bob Hope's radio show, *The Pepsodent Show Starring Bob Hope*, that Shavelson met Sherwood Schwartz, the youngest writer on the staff, who was dubbed "Robin Hood's Rabbi." Schwartz would later go on to create *Gilligan's Island* and *The Brady Bunch*, thus confirming the Bob Hope radio show as an incubator of talent. It might even rank with *The Show of Shows*, which produced a line of writers that included Mel Brooks and Woody Allen.

Shavelson vividly remembered his first night in Hollywood. He had come west to write a screenplay for one of Bob Hope's first pictures. He rented an apartment and then went to the studio. Hope asked him if he had a place to stay yet, and Mel told him he'd rented an apartment. He asked Shavelson if he was married, and Mel replied, "Not yet." As Shavelson writes:

> That seemed to please him. There was no one to share my apartment with me that lonely evening? I thought he was planning to move in with me, perhaps to save rent, but then I realized he had a large rented house and an unrentable wife in the San Fernando Valley, so there must be some other reason. Then he said, as if I were not brand new to this side of show business, "You won't mind if I borrow the key? I'll leave it in the mailbox when I leave around midnight."

Shavelson ruefully comments that he failed to recognize this as the plot for a blockbuster movie; it was years later that Billy Wilder wrote *The Apartment*. Shavelson gave the key to Hope and wandered the streets of Hollywood until midnight, when he found the key in his mailbox—still warm. Thus the social standing of the comedian and the comedy writer.

Bob Hope was at one extreme of the comedy spectrum—someone who needed writers to be funny. Shavelson tells the story of how Hope would have his writers punch up scripts for his films, carry the jokes folded into his script, and then "ad lib" funny new lines on the set. At the time, Shavelson and the writers were happy to divide up the $5,000 Hope gave them for doing this. Later, Shavelson was hired by Samuel Goldwyn, who expressed his relief that he now had his own Bob Hope writer under contract and wouldn't have to pay Hope the $10,000 he gave him each film to pay his writers for punch-up. There is a reason why Bob Hope became a millionaire.

The comedian and the comedy writer. One has the percs, the other has the jokes. The Hollywood writer is the most highly-paid invisible writer in the world. When novelists are successful, they have an audience that identifies their work and purchases it. Playwrights gain reputations with audiences, as do poets, even if theirs are tiny circles. But no one buys a ticket to a movie or turns on a TV show because of the writer. At least, not consciously. They may know they like a comedy show and enjoy seeing those actors, but they never associate either with the writer of the material.

Audiences believe—they want to believe—that comedians are naturally funny and are responsible for their own wit. Even family members fall into this. Lloyd Schwartz is part of a family comedy dynasty. He is Sherwood Schwartz's son, and his two uncles were also comedy writers. Lloyd tells this story about one of those uncles, Al Schwartz, who wrote for Groucho Marx's *You Bet Your Life*:

Shortly after he got the job, Al's own father asked him what he was doing.

"I'm writing for Groucho Marx."

"No, you're not. He makes up all that."

"No, he has writers and there are scripts."

"No, he makes it all up."

Al brought a script to his father, and he refused to read it. He couldn't bear to think that Groucho wasn't making up everything on the spot.

The point is further confused by the fact that many comedians are indeed brilliant comedy writers. Chaplin, Woody Allen, Mel Brooks, Tina Fey, the Wayans brothers—there's a long list. But almost all of them also rely on other writers. So it gets messy.

Cary Grant and Sophia Loren in a trailer for Houseboat, *1958.*

The entire process of writing television comedy is both driven by individual talent and a group dynamic in the writing room, so the mechanism itself gets hard to pin down. Add to this *The Dick Van Dyke Show* model, which audiences have forever emblazoned in their minds as emblematic of the TV writing process, and the confusion widens. Civilians become convinced that either the comic actors invent everything themselves, or a sort of "group think" mushes the scripts into creation.

There is a germ of truth in that diseased misconception. A single writer (or team) pitches a story idea. If the show runner likes the idea, she fleshes out the story idea a bit and pitches it again. Now she gets feedback from the writing room, writes an outline, gets feedback on that (from successively larger groups of people—the writing room, the executive producer, the studio, the network), revises the outline, and finally writes the first draft of a script. More feedback, a revision (at least one)—and then, at that point in the comedy world (but not in the one-hour drama world), a group of writers do indeed sit around a table punching up the script, adding jokes and refining punch lines.

The tension between the traditional loneliness of an author and the committee-like approach of Hollywood confounds both an audience's sanity and that of the writers. It embodies the issue of importance. Perhaps this is part of the comedy writer's curse when it comes to important awards, such as the Oscars. Comedies are routinely snubbed in the nominations for best screenplay or best adapted screenplay. Indeed, for comedies to gain large-scale acclaim as important films, they must always be more than simply funny; they must contain some note of gravitas. The last comedy to win Best Picture, *Annie Hall*, had a Chekhovian note of melancholy, right down to Woody Allen's proposed initial title, *Anhedonia*. No way that *Bananas* gets a nomination, despite its lasting charms.

Comedians tend to feed this perception by making more serious films as they get older. Chaplin goes from *The Gold Rush* to *Limelight*; Woody Allen from *Take the Money and Run* to *Interiors* and *Match Point*. Mel Shavelson moved from *Houseboat* to *Cast a Giant Shadow*, about the war for Israel's independence, and the made-for-TV miniseries about General Dwight Eisenhower's life, *Ike: The War Years*.

Why do we consider making people laugh trivial? Perhaps because it seems familiar. We all recall a class clown; who remembers a class tragedian? Or perhaps it is because comedy is rooted in the obverse of empathy. Mel Brooks famously observed that seeing a guy fall into a manhole and break his arm is funny; stubbing your own toe is tragic.

Comedy brings the refreshment of objectivity. An event is placed against an Olympian view in which someone distant is doing the dying. In *Bananas*, it's funny to see men rounded up in a Central American dictatorship, holding numbers from a deli counter line and waiting their turn to be executed. It's funny because we don't know any of them. For the scene to turn tragic, we just need a touch of backstory—this man waiting to be executed has a young son who loves him—and our hearts break. But that's so easy, like dying. Comedy is hard.

Mel Shavelson turned to the serious with *Cast a Giant Shadow*, his film about the founding of the state of Israel, starring Kirk Douglas as the American Colonel Mickey Marcus, who commanded units of the Israel Defense Force in the 1948 War. *Cast a Giant Shadow* was at the midpoint of Mel's life, but it began the back nine of his career. He was forty-nine at the time, which has always been old in Hollywood years. Consider this lineup: When Judy Garland made her famous Carnegie Hall comeback, battling back from the verge of death, she was thirty-nine. Clark Gable died at fifty-nine. Carole Lombard achieved legendary status before dying at thirty-three in a plane crash.

Shavelson did have a decade of work that followed *Cast a Giant Shadow*: he created a sitcom based on James Thurber's writings, *The War Between Men and Women*, but it only lasted for a couple of seasons. In 1978 he wrote and directed *Ike: The War Years*, a critical and popular hit starring Robert Duvall as Eisenhower. It was an enor-

Kirk Douglas in a publicity shot from Cast a Giant Shadow, *1966.*

mous success and, as he recounts in his memoir, "I had reached the top of the mountain, both artistically and financially, and there was no place to go but downhill." *Ike* was the last produced script Shavelson wrote alone. He never stopped writing, and his autobiography details good projects run to ground, but this blockbuster hit for ABC marked the end of thirty-five years of Mel's scripts in front of a camera.

There is no mandatory retirement age for writers, and most of us continue to write until the very end. Mel started developing *The Little Bugler* when he was eighty-two. Did he envision it as the film that would get him back in the game? Did he foresee it as a project with commercial legs? Did he just find it a compelling story and, like a racehorse that is led to a starting gate, instinctively began to gallop? All that is left is the black binder with his notes, and outline, and the beginning of the script.

Shavelson's outline for *The Little Bugler* runs seventy-three prose pages, almost equivalent to writing the full screenplay. Why not just write the script? This was the standard old-school method employed by many screenwriters at many studios. It was typical in the 1930s and '40s to write a seventy- to eighty-page prose outline before going to script. It allowed the author to editorialize about the themes of the work, to include research that might never appear on screen, and to read more like a novel. This generation of writers worshipped the novel, and possibly these lengthy outlines were the shadow novels they never got to complete.

Flipping through the thick binder of material that Mel assembled and wrote for *The Little Bugler*, one sees all of the steps that build a film, a sort of primer of a typical screenplay process. It begins with discovering a good story in a nonfiction book. In the back of the binder are copies of reviews of *The Little Bugler*, the biography of Gustav Schurmann, who enlisted in the 40th New York Infantry in 1861, when he was twelve. He saw action in ten Civil War battles and became a friend to Tad Lincoln, President Lincoln's young son.

Following the reviews are emails regarding acquiring an option to the rights for the book. In a letter to his agent, Don Kopaloff, Mel presents what hooked his interest:

> This is the true story of twelve-year-old Gustav A. Schurmann, who served as a musician in Company I, 40th New York Infantry, from 1861-1864. This book vividly depicts all of his remarkable wartime experiences, including his stay at the White House as the boyhood companion of Tod [sic] Lincoln. At the end of Schurmann's distinguished military career at age fifteen, he was a decorated veteran of ten battles—from Bull Run to Gettysburg. The true story is startling in its depiction of the horrors of the Civil War as seen through a child's eye … What it needs, of course, is a structure, a story, and a great deal of invention, focusing on Lincoln's assassination, in which Gus and Tad were involved with John Wilkes Booth, the assassin, before the crime.

Structure, which is synonymous with story in filmmaking, is always the writer's preoccupation. The hook of a child's-eye view of the Civil War is powerful, but it needs to be shaped into a story that is more than a string of battles and episodes and propels the hero forward through three acts.

Having secured the rights, the next step is research. The binder offers an opportunity to see a veteran writer on the prowl, digging through history to find his three acts. There are dozens of pages from Civil War accounts; a copy of Mark Twain's short sketch, "The Private History of a Campaign That Failed"; and printouts from

Civil War battlefield visitor centers. One piece of research, which Tony Kushner also found a visual winner and incorporated into his 2012 film *Lincoln*, relates how little Tad Lincoln raced around the White House in a cart drawn by a goat. Another leads Mel to incorporate the story of a rebel spy, Rose Greenow, "Rebel Rose." He obviously thought the addition of Rebel Rose offered conflict and romance. There are pages of notes on her, and random ideas for scenes or dramatic set-pieces:

> Cabinet meeting in the White House. Information—Manassas Junction—they have drawn up a plan. Meeting breaks up, urgent meeting with Rose Greenow, and a delegation of women, begging him not to continue a war that may destroy a country, many women like her from the South in Washington … Tad comes in with goat cart?

There is a page of possible openings:

> OPEN WITH ATTACK AND SURRENDER AT FT. SUMTER.
>
> SCENE AT WHITE HOUSE—LINCOLN AND CABINET—TAD BREAKS IN? GOAT? Lincoln enlists Tad to behave for the duration? Mrs. Lincoln follows him in? …
>
> NEWSPAPER HEADLINE: FT. SUMTER ATTACKED; LINCOLN CALLS FOR 75,000 VOLUNTEERS. Pull back camera, see headline being sold by newsboy—Gus. Father tells him he is going to enlist—Gus insists on going, too.

There are notes from Stephen Crane's novel *The Red Badge of Courage* and notes from Rob Reiner's film *Stand By Me*, always a touchstone when doing a coming-of-age story. There are a couple of pages about black drummers in the United States Colored Troops (USCT) during the war, and some pondering about including a black drummer boy as a friend for Gus. There's a breakdown of each chapter of *The Little Bugler*. There are some of Lincoln's great lines: "No man has a good enough memory to make a successful liar … Few can be induced to labor exclusively for posterity; posterity has done nothing for us … I have been told I was on the road to Hell, but I had no idea it was a mile down the road with a dome on it."

Sandwiched in between all this, I find a two-page "Possible Story line." And then there is the first page of "THE LITTLE BUGLER: First Draft Treatment":

> Did you ever see a freckle-faced kid get his head blown off at your side when you were 12 years old? Did all your childhood dreams about the glory of war vanish when a bullet blew your bugle out of your mouth and killed your father? And did you still remain your own Huckleberry Finn at heart, still manage to retain your boyish laughter and mischievous nature and love of music, and become the symbol of the goodness of humanity that could not be destroyed even in a bloody war? And did that help you to ease the terrible burden on the shoulders of a troubled President who had become your friend? It happened. It all happened to a small boy named Gustav Schurmann, "Gus" to his friends and to his President …

This is a solid pitch, the strong sales job required to push through the enormous project of getting a movie off the ground. Then, two pages later, Mel Shavelson's introductory pages end this way:

> What follows here is what has been dimly remembered through the mists of time. Some of it is factual, some of it is fiction. No man is around to challenge which is which, since Gus kept no diary. To a child, life is largely a dream, to be forgotten as soon as we grow up and learn to lie about it.

The black binder holds the most recent work on top—the first pages of the screenplay. Behind that is the lengthy scenario, then back to shorter outlines, back further in time, digging down through the paper trail to "One Line Story Line—The Little Bugler September 20, 1999."

The script begins, reading well through page 15, then suddenly the next page is 74. Then 77. Then 27 through 29, then 46, then 52 through 64, with some deletions, and we are back to the outline. Pages have been lost. Gone forever now. Was there once a complete first draft? Did Mel get to a certain point—page 77 seems to be the farthest stretch of scripted dialogue page—and then stop? Was he working on this when he died? This script is not the Unfinished Symphony, to be completed by another writer. These pages are as dead as the hand that wrote them—they will change no more. They have no importance—if one accepts that the script itself has no importance.

All this work—the research, the thought, the diligence of getting an option, the outlining, the construction—was it all meaningless? An intense effort resulted in a creative product, and this thick binder now stands as a *memento mori* for all writers. As we all write our scripts, as I pass every Starbucks and see through its windows the ubiquitous screenwriter tapping dialogue into a laptop (how many thousands of those writers exist in Los Angeles? Every coffee shop is filled with them, churning out thousands of scripts each year), one must ask: is there value in the effort itself, in the pages of a script on a hard drive, or does it achieve value only if it survives the author's death? Why do any of us write, if not for the hope that people will see our work after we are dead?

The pages of *The Little Bugler* are on my desk, filled with Mel's notations, corrections, and attempts to get this thing right. That was important to him. Mel Shavelson was immensely successful. He was nominated for two Oscars. He served three terms as President of the Writers Guild of America, West. He wrote, either by himself or in collaboration, over thirty-five films. He directed twelve movies. And yet … was Mel Shavelson important?

The matter of *importance* in Hollywood defines all of us here. It is a metaphysical rumination—who is important, how important is he or she, is that importance trending uphill or down? Attention in Hollywood translates into importance. Attention and importance are immutably intertwined in this industry. If attention is not being paid to you, you are beneath Willy Loman's STARmeter ranking. And if attention is being paid, you are important.

It hardly matters if your talents are those of Snookie or of Tony Kushner; it is the eyeballs upon you that count. To attract attention is to be important, and to be important is to wield power, to achieve financial security, to leave behind an immutable legacy in film. For screenwriters, this issue of importance must be settled during their lifetime. Unlike authors of prose or poetry, a screenwriter will never be important if his or her scripts are not produced.

Emily Dickinson published fewer than a dozen poems during her lifetime, but the poetry she left behind, championed decades after her death, achieved for her a lasting fame. This is not possible for a screenwriter. Screenwriters draft blueprints for a film, and without the film, a screenplay is at best a writing sample. No screenwriter died anonymously, leaving behind a stack of unproduced scripts that were eventually discovered, made into films, and gave that obscure genius post-mortem fame. (There is actually no reason this couldn't happen; it is possible that a brilliant writer has squirreled away dozens of unproduced screenplays and his young nephew, an aspiring agent, discovers them and promotes them and they are made into hit films—it could happen; I'm just saying it has never happened, probably because Hollywood reveres what is current, what is up-and-coming, and there's no sizzle to be found in a dead writer.)

This helps illustrate why the screenplay is not literature. Literature may be discovered independently of an author and reinterpreted by each generation. Screenplays are a blueprint for collaboration, a sketch of a vision that cannot live without actors, a director, an art director, an editor, an AD, a DP. It is the fate of most screenwriters to become unimportant.

When I die, I will leave behind no head shot, no sign of my smiling face; the writer's head shot, pipe in hand, urbane, sophisticated, is out of fashion. At the garage sale after I am dead, will anyone buy a copy of my scripts? I look at the black binder that holds *The Little Bugler*. Was this story just a commercial idea that struck Mel Shavelson as potentially profitable? Or was there something more?

I am convinced that every notion that gets pitched in Hollywood—at least those by successful professional writers—comes from some point of passion within the writer. As seemingly crass and commercial as the finished product may appear onscreen, if a studio says to its marketing team, "We can sell Smurfs," I can assure you that at the beginning there was some writer who said, "Smurfs speak to me because essentially they are gentle socialists and that's who I am." So how did *The Little Bugler* speak to Melville Shavelson?

The Archive of American Television website features interviews with dozens of writers. Mel is among them. In his interview, he is asked how he'd like to be remembered. He scoffs. "Oh, come on…" Then he adds:

> I know the world too well and the shortness of its memory. The good that men do is oft interred with its bones. I suppose so. I've been fortunate that I haven't had to scramble for a living. Success came early—after my ulcer—I'm happy that I did what I did when I did it, and I'd still like to be doing it.

Nearing ninety, Mel still lived to be making movies. He comments that the audience for his kind of material—call it family entertainment—has shifted; there may no longer be the critical mass required to bring a large enough audience to his kind of movie. And then he addresses the question of the importance of his films:

> There are things that you can't explain their importance to anyone else. A lot of these movies were important to me because of their relation to my own life. The

important thing about a motion picture is that it lives longer than almost anything else … It will live after I'm forgotten. To me, when I see those pictures and I see the actors, I say to myself, "Those actors—how fortunate they are—they'll never get any older." The public remembers them for the best things they did. Cary Grant—when he got older, he refused to make motion pictures. He didn't want to be remembered as that. He didn't know he'd keep getting better looking. He kicked himself because he could have been making pictures until the end. I want to be remembered for the good things I did. These pictures I made 20, 30, 40 years ago, they still get seen today.

Hollywood offers immortality, even to those who are not on the screen. The writers get older, they get gray, they die—but in a hundred years, someone will watch a movie about the founding of Israel, or a houseboat, or the Seven Little Foys—and whatever secret element that drove Mel Shavelson to write that story will be handed on.

What was there about the story of a little bugler that captured Mel's attention, that made him wish to hand it on to posterity? It is the story of a child with a propensity for music, a performer who is thrust into an immense battleground where his illusions are literally blown up before his eyes. Perhaps Mel conjured a twelve-year-old kid's dreams of greatness, a time when a child in Brooklyn imagined befriending legendary American figures like Jimmy Cagney and Bob Hope. A time when he dreamed of breaking out of Brooklyn and someday becoming important.

Through all the years, through the indignities of loaning Bob Hope his apartment for an assignation, through rejections of scripts, through battles with the Israeli army and studio chiefs, in this script that he is constructing in his mind and storing in a black binder, Mel Shavelson identifies with the little bugler. In his final years, Mel remains his own Huckleberry Finn at heart. He somehow manages to retain his boyish laughter, and, in his dreams, posterity views him as the symbol of the goodness of humanity that could not be destroyed, not even by Hollywood.

Samuel Goldwyn, 1962

Samuel Goldwyn's Birthday Party:
A Contact Sheet by Leigh Wiener

IN 1895, THIRTEEN-YEAR-OLD ORPHAN SCHMUEL GELBFISZ walked from his family home in Warsaw 300 miles to the Oder River. He had just the clothes on his back and a small amount of money from selling his deceased father's old suits. He bribed a border official to get into Germany and walked another 200 miles to Hamburg. From there he made his way to London, where he Anglicized his name to Samuel Goldfish.

He eventually reached his ultimate destination: America, where he worked his way up in the glove manufacturing industry to become a top salesman based in Gloversville, New York. On the eve of his eightieth birthday, he was feted by the biggest stars in Hollywood as Samuel Goldwyn, Oscar-winning producer, pioneering filmmaker, and one of Hollywood's founding pillars. He got there as he had left Poland years earlier—alone, with dogged determination.

In 1910, young Sam Goldfish met Blanche Lasky; her brother Jesse was a well-known vaudevillian. Goldfish fell in love and proposed marriage to Blanche. Jesse asked his friend Louis B. Mayer, who owned theaters in Massachusetts, if he knew of Goldfish. Mayer said Lasky should break up the wedding plans because Goldfish was not fit to be the husband of any man's sister. But Goldfish won out, and the marriage took place in a brownstone in New York City.

→ 21

Three years later, Goldfish joined with Lasky and an aspiring theatrical writer and director named Cecil B. DeMille to form a company to make motion pictures. Goldfish was convinced there was a market for full-length movies, ones with real quality. They purchased the rights to the stage play *The Squaw Man,* and DeMille and a small troupe set out to Arizona to film the movie. When they arrived in Flagstaff, it looked flat and dull, and DeMille decided to push on to California. They telegrammed Lasky back in New York: "FLAGSTAFF NO GOOD FOR OUR PURPOSE. HAVE PROCEEDED TO CALIFORNIA. WANT AUTHORITY TO RENT BARN IN PLACE CALLED HOLLYWOOD FOR $75 A MONTH."

As DeMille shot *The Squaw Man,* he cast a child actor, Pat Moore, in a plum role. Pat's younger brother, Micky Moore, visited the set and was photographed there with his brother and actress Anne Little. Micky would go on to work in film for over eighty years.

The Squaw Man was an enormous success, but within a couple of years, Goldfish and his partners had a falling out and he was summarily ejected from the company. This began a lifelong pattern of dissolving partnerships. The next was with playwright Edgar Selwyn. Goldfish knew his name was ridiculed, so for the new company he and Selwyn formed, they combined their names to make Goldwyn. Then he had his name legally changed to Samuel Goldwyn, so it appeared the company was all his.

He joined or started, then left companies that became the cornerstones of Hollywood—Paramount, Metro-Goldwyn-Mayer (despite his name, he never produced for MGM), United Artists. He emerged as the ultimate loner, the producer who insisted on quality in the films he made, just as he had in the gloves he had once sold. He hired the finest writers (Sidney Howard, Ben Hecht, Lillian Hellman), the best directors (John Ford, King Vidor, William Wyler) and actors (Laurence Olivier, Gary Cooper, Merle Oberon, David Niven).

Juxtaposed against his desire for class was his own idiomatic personality. Screenwriter Philip Yordan remembers writing a scene for Goldwyn in which a young man looks at a prostitute who lives in his building, feels aroused, and runs out of the room. Goldwyn confronted him, saying:

> Ah! Disgusting! I vomited! I vomited right on the floor when I read that scene! How can you write such a degenerate scene? I'm gonna have to hire psychiatrists to help you, my boy! That's so filthy! I gave it to my secretary—she threw up!

Yordan was unable to write for the next three days. Then Goldwyn reappeared in his office, closed the door, placed his chair against it, sat down, and told him to write the script. Yordan objected, saying Goldwyn didn't like what he was doing. Goldwyn replied:

> I'll tell you why you're gonna write this script. I'm a rich man. I'm paying you three thousand dollars a week. And you're gonna sit here. I just did *The Best Years of Our Lives,* which made $11 million, so I can afford it. I'll make other pictures, while you sit here on your weekly salary for five years, because I've got a week-to-week contract with you, and as long as I pay you, you have to work on this script. I can demand as many changes of you as I want. After five years, I'm gonna come in on a Monday morning and fire you. Then, you can call your agent. He will tell you Yordan is never going to be offered another job. They will ask: "What has Yordan done the past five years? He has disappeared. You'll never work again …"

Yordan wrote the script.

For all his bullying and bludgeoning, Goldwyn was also a visionary. He wrote an article in 1949 entitled "Hollywood in the Television Age" (rather, he had one of his writers draft a version of his ideas). The concept he put forth must have seemed impossible, even laughable at the time—some sixty-five years ago. Goldwyn wrote:

> [There] remains the problem of how the motion picture industry is going to receive financial returns for pictures made for television. The greatest potentialities lie in a device called phonevision.

> This device is not yet known to the American public because it has not yet been placed upon the commercial market, but to motion picture producers it may well be the key to full participation in this new, exciting medium of entertainment. Reduced to its simplest terms, it is a system by which any television-set owner will be able to call his telephone operator, tell her that he wishes to see *The Best Years of Our Lives* (if I may be pardoned for thinking of my favorite picture), or any other picture, and then see the picture on his television set. The charge for the showing of the picture will be carried on the regular monthly telephone bill.

> Phonevision is normal television with the additional feature that it can be seen on the phonevision-television combination set only when certain electric sig-

nals are fed into the set over telephone wires. No television set without the phonevision addition is capable of picking up phonevision programs, and no phonevision-television set can pick up such programs without those electrical signals supplied over the telephone wires on specific order.

The fee paid by the set owner will presumably be divided between the television transmitter, the picture producer, and the telephone company. The range of possibilities which this prospect opens to motion picture producers is almost limitless, for every television owner becomes just as much a box-office prospect inside his home as outside it.

On August 26, 1962, Goldwyn's eightieth birthday, the royalty of Hollywood gathered for a dinner in his honor. The tables were filled with carnations, as if the guests were attending a memorial service for someone who didn't want to pay for lilies. This created a floating cloud of flowers that bordered the faces of all the stars. The men smoked cigars; the smaller their current stature in the business, the larger the cigar. George Jessel sported an enormous stogie; Frank Sinatra had none. Leigh Wiener was there and captured all the smiling and laughing faces: Sinatra, Jimmy Stewart, Eddie Fisher, Shirley Jones, Milton Berle, Harpo Marx. And glowering at them all was Schmuel Gelbfisz.

Harpo  Marx

WHEN I WAS A CHILD GROWING UP IN COLUMBIA, MISSOURI, my favorite book was *Harpo Speaks*. It had been given to our family by Hal Swenson, an eccentric philosophy professor who looked and behaved quite a bit like Harpo's good friend Alexander Woollcott, the portly critic and wit of the Algonquin Circle. *Harpo Speaks* transported me to the world of New York in the 1920s, filled with

Broadway shows, the Thanatopsis Club's endless weekend poker sessions, croquet games atop penthouses, crazy nights on Long Island, and Harpo acting generally like a genial idiot, stripping nude when it suited him, eating flowers, standing on his head, soaking in the great city.

He behaved like a Dada artist. Once he and his brother Chico decided to sell money to a policeman. They offered him a dollar bill for the special price of ninety cents. Then they offered him a two-dollar bill for a dollar seventy. Finally, when they offered him a five-dollar bill for four-fifty, he had had enough and threatened to haul them in, insisting they must have some sort of racket going on. "No racket," said Chico. "We just like to sell money." The cop walked away, muttering they were nuts.

The Marx brothers were masters of anarchy, which is their enduring appeal. When Groucho said, "You can't burn the candle at both ends," and Harpo reached into his coat and pulled out a candle burning at both ends—well, that summed up a joyous youthful celebration that all the old bromides about life were really bullshit.

Harpo invested his passion in things like games of "Murder," in which a designated party guest of the "murderer" would silently tell George S. Kaufman or Dorothy Parker that she was "dead." Then, when the body was found, a designated judge would attempt to deduce the murderer. There were croquet games with Woollcott, who, after a particularly good shot in their summer games on Neshobe Island, would kick his heels together and sing, "I'm des a 'itto wabbit in de sunshine! / I'm des a 'itto bunny in de wain!" Harpo laments in his book:

> It's sad to realize that today [in 1961], when there's supposed to be more of everything, there are no more wabbits in de sunshine or bunnies in de wain. Famous Persons, anagrams, Murder, and croquet are lost in the TV shuffle, and that's an awful shame. My God, those games were fun!

In short, the 1920s were a decade when Harpo and his friends were gloriously crazed children. When he moved to Hollywood, things seemed to quiet down, especially after he married actress Susan Fleming and children entered the picture; family life is always a sedative in biographies.

In *Harpo Speaks,* he describes a dinner at David O. Selznick's home in 1940 with Rose and Ben Hecht and Dr. Sam Hirshfeld. The talk turned to psychoanalysis, which was the rage in Hollywood. Rose Hecht asked for silence, pointed to Harpo, and said, "There sits the only normal man in Hollywood." She backed up her statement with: "He's never taken a sleeping pill. He's not money-mad or driven by ambition. He's mature. He's adjusted. He's a breath of fresh air in a town full of neurotic exhibitions and show-offs." When Harpo died of a heart attack in 1964 at his home in Rancho Mirage, Rose Hecht's analysis was still sadly true for those of us who love the concept of anarchy without having to live it out.

Eddie Fisher

QUICK: name an Eddie Fisher hit. Or, better yet, describe the quality of his voice. Eddie Fisher was a major singing star of the first half of the 1950s, with twenty-four singles in the Top Ten, but compared to the indelible vocal quality of his rivals from 1950 to the dawn of Elvis—Nat King Cole, Frank Sinatra, Tony Bennett—Eddie Fisher draws a blank.

Ever hear his 1953 Number 1 hit, "Oh, My Pa-Pa"? Or his version of "I'm Walking Behind You," a song that both he and Sinatra recorded, but his was the more popular? He had his own weekly NBC television show for four years, *Coke Time with Eddie Fisher*—not a title that would get you on the air today, but when does public television use those broadcasts as fundraisers?

Eddie Fisher is remembered today for one thing: he was a home wrecker. He was married to Debbie Reynolds, and their daughter Carrie Fisher describes in shorthand what happened:

Mom and Dad were great friends with Elizabeth Taylor and her husband Mike Todd. Mike died in a plane crash in 1958, when I was two, and my dad flew to Elizabeth's side, making his way slowly to her front. He first dried her eyes with his handkerchief, then he consoled her with flowers, and he ultimately consoled her with his penis.

So Fisher left Debbie Reynolds to marry Elizabeth Taylor. Taylor then dumped him to marry Richard Burton. It's a perfectly rational ladder of Darwinian beauty: Liz trumps Debbie Reynolds, and Burton trumps Eddie Fisher. There would also be a rough justice here, except that Fisher never stopped bedding beautiful women. In his autobiography, *Been There, Done That*, he claims to have made the beast with two backs with a list containing:

[Not] just Elizabeth [Taylor] and Connie Stevens and Debbie Reynolds, but sex symbols like Kim Novak and Mamie Van Doren; classic beauties like Marlene Dietrich, who advised me never to marry an actress, and Merle Oberon; movie stars like Ann-Margret and Angie Dickinson, Stefanie Powers and Sue Lyon, who wanted to compare my sexual prowess with Richard Burton's; singers like Abbe Lane, Michele Phillips and Dinah Shore, even women of controversy like Judith Exner, who also had long-lasting affairs with my friend the Mafia boss Sam Giancana and President Kennedy, and Pam Turnure, Jackie Kennedy's press secretary.

As the poet says, one can either make a life in art or art of one's life, and Fisher chose to paint on a palette of pudenda. This, rather than music, was his real passion, and the reason we no longer hear his voice is because he wasn't very serious about singing.

Eddie Fisher grew up in Philadelphia, the son of Russian Jewish immigrants who called him "Sonny Boy," after the song in Al Jolson's movie *The Singing Fool*. He was never trained as a singer, claiming "I never had a singing lesson … I was born in tune. I didn't know flats or sharps, and I couldn't read music. I just opened my mouth and sang." And he never worked at the craft of singing:

Frank [Sinatra] was the chairman of the board; I could have been at least the CEO. But I was too lazy, too interested in other things. Sinatra made it look easy, Bing [Crosby] made it look easy, Perry Como made it look easy. It took them a lot of hard work to make it look so easy. Singing is hard work. It's getting involved in what you do. Hit records are fine and I certainly had my share of them—more than my share. But it was all bubble-gum music, and it lost its taste pretty fast.

But the public's taste for Eddie Fisher did not go away, at least not that of the female public:

There were models and Playboy Playmates and New York showgirls, Las Vegas chorus girls and beauty queens. I didn't even have to pursue them; gorgeous women were constantly coming on to me. Men used to hang around with me just to get my castoffs.

Carrie Fisher wrote that after reading her father's autobiography, "I wanted to get my DNA fumigated."

Eddie Fisher was addicted to drugs and gambling, something which he acknowledged in his memoir, but his addiction to women is trumpeted, not diagnosed. Hollywood was built on sex; sex sells movies, stars usually rely on some form of sex appeal, and God knows the American habit of selling commercial products through sex has never gone away. Perhaps Eddie Fisher chose to cultivate his sexual prowess instead of his talent because it was as American as apple pie.

And there he sits at the dinner saluting Samuel Goldwyn, a man who refused to come near to any mention of real sex in his films. It is a classic Hollywood dichotomy: the obsession with sex, and the obsession to shield the rest of America from it.

SAMUEL GOLDWYN'S BIRTHDAY

George Jessel

ACTOR, SONGWRITER, SINGER, AND COMEDIAN George Jessel earned his nickname, "Toastmaster General of the United States," by frequently serving as emcee at political and entertainment gatherings. He was especially famous for his eulogies, which ring with nineteenth-century diction. His eulogy for Al Jolson, delivered at Temple Israel on Hollywood Boulevard on October 26, 1950, begins this way:

> A breeze from San Francisco Bay and the life of the greatest minstrel America has ever known is in the balance. A turn of a card—a telling of a gag—and within a few moments, a wife, a legion of admirers, and a nation are broken-hearted. So it was—and so, alas, it is—the passing from this earthly scene of Al Jolson. And the voice that put majesty into the American popular song must from now on come from a disc instead of a heart, from whence it came.

And on it goes, a stem-winder that no longer appeals through its florid prose.

It was probably in Jessel's bones, the urge for the dramatic; his mother was a ticket seller at the Imperial Theater in New York, and he was a child usher. She formed a singing group of child ushers that included him and Walter Winchell. Later, George partnered with a young Eddie Cantor as child comedians until George outgrew the role at sixteen. He appeared in vaudeville doing a famous routine in which the audience sees only his side of a phone conversation with his mother. He co-wrote lyrics for a hit song, "Oh How I Laugh When I Think How I Cried About You." Then he was cast on Broadway in the starring role of *The Jazz Singer*. When Warner Brothers got ready to make the movie, he asked for too much money and they turned to Al Jolson. The movie catapulted Jolson to new heights of fame, and Jessel went on to play smaller roles.

He began producing musicals for Fox and did well through the 1940s into the 1960s. He was a founding member of the Friars Club and became famous on the Hollywood banquet circuit, throwing amiable barbs at fellow celebrities. He held no bitterness toward Al Jolson's fortune and revered him to the end. Although he was honest in his assessment:

> You can't say that Jolson was an egocentric. Most men love themselves—and I believe it was La Rochefoucauld or Ed Sullivan who said: "A man must love himself, for this is the only lifelong romance." Egocentric is too small a word for Jolson … He was only content while singing and acknowledging applause; the rest of the time he was champing at the bit while getting ready to go on—and if he was not on, he was disconsolate.

Jessel threatened to tape-record his own eulogy and thus deliver it himself. He did dictate what should appear on his tombstone: "I tell you here from the shade it is all worthwhile.'" His old friend Milton Berle delivered Jessel's eulogy in May of 1981.

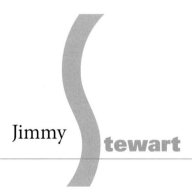

Jimmy Stewart

A FRIEND OF MINE attended All Saints' Episcopal Church in Beverly Hills. She described her shock one day many years ago when the moment in the service arrived to greet your neighbors. The gentleman in front of her turned around, extended his hand, and stuttered, "P-p-peace be with you." It was Jimmy Stewart.

He was Hollywood's most unassuming star. When he took on *Hawkins*, a television series in the 1970s, the show's creator, David Karp, asked his son to greet Stewart as he entered MGM to film the pilot. The son came back confused; he couldn't find him. Instead of driving a fancy convertible, Jimmy Stewart had

walked in without his hairpiece and carrying a lunch pail. He looked like a grip.

Jimmy Stewart made the craft of acting look effortless. We in the audience always assumed that somehow the cameras had been turned on and he just stepped forward and spoke his lines as he would in real life, and what you saw was exactly what Jimmy Stewart was—the decent, self-effacing, lanky guy from Indiana, Pennsylvania. The truth was that he was a hard-working actor, one who was very conscious of his craft. Director Jud Taylor remembered Stewart's preparation for *Hawkins*:

> When it came to shooting, he was letter-perfect. And he did something I've never seen before or since. After we blocked a scene and the technicians would be lighting it, very often he would continue to do his lines and action instead of the stand-in. And I said to him, "Jim, why don't you go and sit down." And he said, "I have to get all this business down so I can forget about it."

He was the consummate professional and a man everyone could trust. When Jack Warner heard that Ronald Reagan was going to run for governor of California, he said, "No, Jimmy Stewart for governor. Ronald Reagan for best friend."

Milton Berle

IN 1950, eighty percent of Americans watched Milton Berle each week on *Texaco Star Theater*. Movie theaters noticed a pronounced drop in attendance on Tuesday nights when the show aired, and restaurants closed early. The city of Detroit reported a mysterious and enormous drop in water usage for an hour on Tuesday nights: people waited to use the bathroom until after the program ended.

Milton Berle was "Mr. Television," and his stardom was a phenomenon that defined the addictive power of television. Ten years later, he was the host of *Jackpot Bowling*, which went off the air within a year. Such is the nature of television's gold-rush mentality: the lucky strike carries outrageously good fortune, and then the dizzying fall comes just as quickly.

Milton Berle was born in Manhattan, the son of paint and varnish salesman Moses Berlinger and his wife, Sadie. He was a child actor, appearing in silent movies, many of which were then being shot in New Jersey. In his autobiography, he claims that while he was working on in his first film, *The Perils of Pauline,* the director told him he would be thrown from a moving train:

> I was scared shitless, even when he went on to tell me that Pauline would save my life. Which is exactly what happened, except that at the crucial moment they threw a bundle of rags instead of me from the train. I bet there are a lot of comedians around today who are sorry about that.

He worked his way up through vaudeville, and in many respects never left that broad comic background. Indeed, much of what America loved on the *Texaco Star Theater* was material lifted from his vaudeville days, including the cross-dressing comedy.

He was not an easy man. His son, William Berle, wrote a biography of his father, detailing how "Uncle Miltie" hired a prostitute for him when he was sixteen, and how, at the memorial service for his second wife, Ruth Cosgrove, Milton Berle told jokes and never mentioned her name. He was addicted to gambling and an ar-

dent womanizer who was famously rumored to be the most well-endowed man in Hollywood. In Truman Capote's short story "A Beautiful Child," Marilyn Monroe remarks, "Everybody says Milton Berle has the biggest schlong in Hollywood," and at the New York Friars Club memorial service for Berle, the comic Freddie Roman said, "On May 1st and May 2nd, his penis will be buried."

For a time, no one's star burned brighter, and then in the 1960s he defined the word "has-been." He proved himself a good actor in small roles, including the starring role in The *Dick Powell Show* drama "Doyle Against the House," in which he played a gambler. In 1979, he infamously guest-hosted *Saturday Night Live,* taking control of the show unannounced, mugging, and ending with an unauthorized singing of "September Song." Producer Lorne Michaels banned him from ever appearing again.

Berle's third wife, Lorna, alienated the children and then had Berle buried at Hillside Memorial Park instead of the double crypt at Mount Sinai where he had planned to be interred with his second wife, Ruth. Bill Berle said at the time, "It happens to be where Al Jolson was buried, and my father and Mr. Jolson were not exactly friends. His memory's being disrespected."

Bill Berle once wrote this summary of his father's life for a celebrity death website that included misinformation about Milton Berle's funeral. It might read as a metaphor for the medium of television:

Milton Berle was an over-achiever and an under-achiever, he was the greatest in the world at some things and the worst at others. What too few people understand is that like other historical figures, he gave up almost everything else in life to be the greatest at one thing. His should be both an inspirational tale and a cautionary tale, a great tragedy as much as a success story. By all rights you should love him and hate him, as I did.

Shirley Jones

SHIRLEY JONES CEMENTED HER RELATIONSHIP with the American public as the girl/Mom next door with her starring role in *The Partridge Family*. Was that a step down from starring in the film versions of *Oklahoma!*, *Carousel*, and *The Music Man*? Without a doubt. She realized the dangerous career detour she was taking:

> The problem with *Partridge*—though it was great for me and gave me an opportunity to stay home and raise my kids—when my agents came to me and presented it to me, they said if you do a series and it becomes a hit show, you will be that character for the rest of your life and your movie career will go into the toilet, which is what happened. But I have no regrets.

One accidental piece of casting for the show helped convince the world that this was a family decision: her stepson, David Cassidy, played the role of Keith Partridge. Amazingly, the casting director and network had no idea they were related. David has told the story:

> At the auditions, they introduced me to the lead actress (Shirley Jones) 'cause they had no idea, they had no idea. So I said, "What are you doing here?" She looked at me and said, "What are you doing here?" And I said, "Well, I'm reading for the lead guy." I said, "What are you doing here?" She said, "I'm the mother!"

Shirley Jones had arrived in New York as a young singer from Pennsylvania. She auditioned for Richard Rodgers, who was so impressed that he rushed Oscar Hammerstein over to see her audition, too, and she ended up being the only actress ever under personal contract to that great team. She played minor roles in *South Pacific* and *Me and Juliet,* and then Rodgers and Hammerstein lobbied for her to take the lead in the film version of *Carousel.* Frank Sinatra was going to be her leading man, but he dropped out when he learned that each scene would be shot twice to accommodate Cinemascope technology. His theory was that he should be paid twice because he was shooting one film in 35 mm and another in 55 mm. Somehow the studio didn't see it that way and replaced him with Gordon MacRae.

Jones projected All-American sweetness and blondeness, and then, in 1959, she was cast against type in *Elmer Gantry.* Hollywood loves playing against type. In this Richard Brooks film, Jones was a hooker who had been involved with Burt Lancaster's Gantry years earlier—and won an Oscar for her performance.

She had a somewhat tumultuous marriage to actor Jack Cassidy, whom she started seeing when she was twenty. Cassidy, she told a reporter, taught her about "absolutely everything. I learned about life with Jack, about parties with Jack, drinking with Jack, design with Jack. He was bright, well-read, smart." They were separated and she was living in Los Angeles doing *The Partridge Family* when, on December 11, 1976, Cassidy fell asleep on the couch of his penthouse holding a lit cigarette. He died in the blaze.

In 1977, Shirley Jones married comic and actor Marty Ingels. It seemed like a step from New York urbanity (Cassidy, for instance, had a premarital sexual encounter with Cole Porter) to Burbank television humor; Ingels once appeared for an interview wearing a purple bathrobe and an oversized hat labeled "HUSBAND," cracking jokes about being kept in the attic.

There is a death grip about television, especially successful television. The American public freezes you in a moment and a role and there you are, a sort of media stalactite, hanging from the darkened cave of the television set, beautiful to view but unchanging to the human eye. Shirley Jones knew this going into the little box that lives in American homes; she knew she was giving up forever whatever dark corner allowed her to play a vengeful hooker. We may appreciate her work as Lulu Bains in *Elmer Gantry,* but that will stand only as counter-programming to the Shirley Partridge in our minds.

Frank Sinatra

ONE OF MY EARLY AND STARTLING DISCOVERIES about Los Angeles culture is that the gossip columns here are embedded in the real-estate news. Coming from New York and Page Six of the *Post*, I was initially confused when I leafed through the *Los Angeles Times*. Where was the gossip column? Maybe, I thought, this paper was more elevated than the New York tabloids; it seemed to have more in common with the *Times* than the *Daily News*.

Then one Sunday I came across the "Hot Property" real-estate column. It listed homes for sale, but much more: Madonna was selling her Malibu beach house because of her marriage was on the fritz. Jennifer Aniston was purchasing a Pacific Palisades charmer to accommodate the new love interest in her life. Bruce Springsteen's extended tour meant his Beverly Hills Tudor would be on the market.

Of course. Gossip in Los Angeles is inextricably linked to real estate. In a material culture, where we live makes the ultimate statement of personal worth. We can say that Hollywood is all about the movies, but it is also all about real estate. Far more fortunes have been made here—lasting fortunes—by people smart enough to buy when the market is low and sell when the market is high.

Frank Sinatra's name came up frequently. It seems as though he had an endless stream of homes he was buying, selling, leasing, renting. Sinatra's Holmby Hills mansion was on the market; Sinatra's Palm Desert getaway was for sale; Sinatra's former estate in Chatsworth, the fabled Farralone, was coming on the market.

It was the word "Chatsworth" that arrested my attention. In the sprawling mega-metropolis that is Los Angeles, Chatsworth is a city between the West Valley and Malibu. Or, more properly, it once was a completely independent little town near the Malibu coastline, which has now been threatened by urban creep from the San Fernando Valley. At any rate, it seemed like a strange place for Frank Sinatra to have an estate.

Then I read of Farralone in realtor Lynn Teschner's advertisement. In the purple prose of real estate, which I admit is a guilty pleasure:

It has been referred to as "The great glass mansion that perches like a lighted jewel on its own 13.5 acre hilltop." No wonder, with its 16 ft. ceilings the interior is surrounded by glass walls that open seamlessly to the outdoor spaces. Today the property has been painstakingly restored to its pristine original condition and continues to sparkle and amaze.

The estate known as "Farralone" was commissioned by Dora Hutchison, the heiress to the Chase Manhattan Bank fortune. It was completed in 1951 by Pereira & Luckman, the architects most famous for building this "trophy" residence, The Los Angeles County Museum of Art, the Kennedy Center, the Transamerica Pyramid building in San Francisco, and the master plan for the City of Beverly Hills.

The parties hosted there between 1951-1954 were legendary and included such guests as Lucille Ball and Ava Gardner. Judy Garland and Vincente Minnelli renewed their wedding vows there. Frank Sinatra leased the house for several years. During that time, Marilyn Monroe frequently resided in the guesthouse. She had one of her last photo shoots there, as well as her alleged rendezvous with Jack Kennedy.

Sinatra rented the home during his 1950s Rat Pack days and sublet the guesthouse to Marilyn Monroe. The most famous and charged coupling of the century—the President and the movie star—occurred in Chatsworth? The incongruity of it somehow perfectly matches Los Angeles and Frank Sinatra. Elegance is portable in this world, as easily plopped down as a movie set raised in the middle of the night in a godforsaken plain of the west Valley. For the week it stands, it represents the height of contemporary fashion and architecture. Why not stick an architectural landmark out in the middle of a dusty range of foothills? It's Hollywood. It exists outside of context, a construction made for a glass bubble. As Frank taught us, class is something you can carry in a suitcase.

PROVIDENCE   EP. 303   "The Red Shoes"   Writer's Draft   8/7/00   8.

3   CONTINUED: 3

                    JOANIE
          You know, it's a process.

                    BERT
          Right.

                    JOANIE
          One time doesn't mean anything. *misleading*

                    BERT
               (half-heartedly)
          Yeah.

                    JOANIE
          It's only in romance novels that
          there's fireworks and... whatever.

                    BERT
          Sure.

     A beat.

                    JOANIE
          Can you hug me?

     Bert turns and puts his arm around Joanie. Neither one looks
     reassured. We PUSH IN on Joanie's naked back and

                                        MATCH DISSOLVE TO:

4   INT. JOHN'S OFFICE - DAY   *(do this later) → while she ponders*
                                       whether to call him or following
     CLOSE ON SYD'S NAKED BACK   *keep (on him)*

     Dotted with acupuncture needles. John deftly places another.   X

                    SYD   *For first time, roles are*
          Is it in?   *reversed - John's in dilemma -*
                                       ache for her help.
                    JOHN   *Listen their smarts &*
               (affirming)   *want to tell to go about.*
          Uh-huh.   *Our relationship is getting*
                                       beyond professional!
                    SYD   *(Syd slightly taken aback -*
          Didn't even feel it.   *but will do it)*

                    JOHN
          Good. Because if you did, you
          wouldn't be in the hands of a
          certified acupuncture therapist.
                    (MORE)

     John - mind if we stop therapy
     this morning -   (CONTINUED)

A page from the writer's draft of a script for Providence, *2000.*

Providence

I HAVE IN MY HANDS fifty-three pieces of paper that changed my life dramatically and forever. They are the shards from my own Hollywood excavation. They are the pages of a script.

A writer always dreams of the one magical script that will catapult him or her to glory, to sizzling success and material wealth. We almost never imagine the reverse—the cursed script whose bite turns the author's career catatonic, putting it to sleep in a version of Hollywood's *Sleeping Beauty*: the body is still visible, but not a breath of dialogue emerges into the air. To look again over these fifty-three pages is to remember the nightmare of a failure.

I am tempting fate to even hint at the word "failure," because saying the F-word out loud in Hollywood is to name Rumpelstiltskin or utter "Voldemort." The Death Eaters will be circling soon, as I have called up the demon that lives beneath the Hollywood Hills. He is a powerful monster, fueling the paranoia of all those who attempt to sleep in the shadow of the studios. He spews endless sulfur deep under Sunset Boulevard, spurring the dark nights of the writer and the lost morning hours of the producer and the high noon of the lonely actor. He is the engine of the ambitious, who flee his shadow; the gigantic worm that burrows ceaselessly below the Avenue of the Stars; the Anti-Christ of Los Angeles, the Lord of the entertainment underworld, and his name is the Great God Failure.

Success

When I first moved to Los Angeles, I marveled at the incredibly high rate of success enjoyed by everyone I met. Each person I spoke with told me, with a thin but enthusiastic smile, about their projects, which were all moving forward in various ways. Just yesterday, a big-name director said he would like to be attached. A major actor was reading the script. A Creative Artists Agency (CAA) agent was passionate about the project. It took me several years to realize that these tales of projects rocketing on an upward trajectory were complete bullshit. But this was bullshit propelled forward as a life-sustaining force; survival technique bullshit, because failure on any level in Hollywood carries with it a carrion stench.

It is no accident that so many self-help gurus have launched their careers in Southern California. The ever-present sunshine seeps into people's souls as a standard to live by. If you are not sunny, if you are not projecting positive energy, rays of success streaming from behind your head and out your ass, you are at odds with the very essence of nature.

Is it a coincidence that just below where the Hollywood sign stands today once stood Krotona, the "place of promise," a settlement of the Theosophical Society's Adyar branch funded by a Virginia lawyer named Albert P. Warrington, which included the Grand Temple of the Rosy Cross, a lotus pond, and an amphitheater where audiences watched Buddha come to life? In 1927, sociologist H. Paul Douglas claimed, "There are in Los Angeles more sects, cults, and denominations than in any other city in the world." They included the Nuptual Feast Ecclesia, the First Assembly of the First Born of the United Sons of the Almighty, and Nothing Impossible. In 1937, author Carey McWilliams wrote:

> In Los Angeles I have attended the services of the Agabeg Occult Church, where the woman pastor had violet hair and green-painted eyelids; of the Great White Brotherhood, whose yellow-robed followers celebrate the full moon of May in a special ritual; of the Ancient Mystical Order of Melchizedek; of the Temple of the Jeweled Cross ...

Utopias blossomed throughout Los Angeles. Arthur Bell's Mankind United was gearing up for a worldwide utopia of universal employment, with everyone working four hours a days, four days a week. This Utopia would follow upon the triumph of the "Sponsors" over the "Hidden Rulers" and "Money Changers," the malevolent conspiracy that ran the world. (The only utopia that resulted was Arthur Bell's short-lived personal pleasure palace, which consisted of a mansion on the Sunset Strip with an indoor swimming pool, pipe organ, and secret cocktail bar.)

Los Angeles was also home to the "I AM" cult, founded in 1929 after Guy Ballard fled to Hollywood after being indicted for stock fraud in Illinois. He self-published *Unveiled Mysteries*, chronicling a hike near Mt. Shasta where he encountered the

Ascended Master Saint Germain. Germain offered him a cup of "pure electronic essence" and a wafer of "concentrated energy" and took him on a journey to ancient Karnak, Luxor, and the cities of the Inca. The "I AM" Activity believes in a group of Ascended Masters who have been reincarnated over hundreds of years, eventually becoming immortal. The Masters communicated to humanity through certain channels, including Guy Ballard and his wife, Edna.

There is a direct line between the eagerness of Los Angelinos to achieve immortality and the movie industry. No other business offers the possibility of unending life in such a concrete fashion. We see the actors of fifty or one hundred years ago flicker on the screen today, still alive in a simulacrum. Film captures their voices, their physicality, their emotions—is this not a kind of pure electronic essence? Immortality is success. Failure is death.

I believe that inability to accept failure accounts for Hollywood's peculiar use of the term "project." Before I arrived in Los Angeles, I didn't understand this term "project." We write scripts, not projects. But over the years, I came to appreciate the saving nomenclature of "project." Once one announces that a script has been written, it exists as an entity available for judgment. The script is great. Or it stinks. Or it is somewhere in between. But it becomes a finished commodity to be placed on the scales of judgment. Completion of a script opens the door, in other words, for failure. But if one is working on a *project*—the ongoing development of a script, the pulling together of talent, the vision of production needs—that implies a living organism of effort that is impossible to mark as failure because it has not yet come to fruition.

It's like working on a housing project. It can take years, and once it is finally erected, adjustments can be made. Until your project becomes the filmic metaphor of Pruitt-Igoe in St. Louis, the embodiment of an ill-conceived disaster, your film project is simply undergoing additional planning, some tinkering, seeking additional funding—it is alive, it is poised for success, it will never become a failure because, in all likelihood, it will never exist.

My wife and I arrived from New York and the world of theater, where failure was an accepted and ennobling experience. Everyone in theater knows that on any given day, you might have to haul the two wooden chairs and table that constitute the set of your play across the streets of the East Village and set them in a tiny performance space and then perform for an audience of six. In addition, theater people tend to embrace willfully introverted pieces, plays which I would say speak to the choir, except they usually speak to about a quartet. And if the quartet doesn't appreciate the play, well, it may just be beyond them. Failure is embraced fully—it's just that it's not our failure, it's the failure of the audience.

We have all sat in Ukrainian coffee shops at midnight, talking through a catastrophe that we've just participated in and parsing the strange silence of our audience. "They were so with us they couldn't breathe." "They were too moved to applaud." "My friend told me afterwards that this is something really special." The fact that in tangible terms—in terms measured by box office receipts and reviews—the play we were all engaged with was a failure of the first order matters not at all. Even if the failure becomes rather famous, a richly told tale of catastrophe like the musical *Carrie*, the tales become the stuff of legend, something that adds luster to a career because one has been through the fire (literally).

Los Angeles, in contrast, doesn't process failure well. When a film bombs, when a TV show fails, there is no commiseration, no mourning, no shared remorse. Instead, a veil of silence is rapidly and permanently drawn across the project—and often its creator. "We are sad that this project never found its audience," one reads in *Variety*, the vapid canned quotation handed down from studio executive to studio executive over the years. (I can guarantee you that there will never be a quotation from a studio executive saying "You know, this show really sucked, so good riddance," because at some point in the future that studio executive might need the creative team responsible for this debacle.) This town has a reflexive reaction to failure, a psychic projectile vomiting to rid oneself of the odious mass of stinking shit that was a failed TV show.

The reverse side of this coin is that everyone touts his or her success. If you have not achieved success, you make it up. This mendacity is of a piece with the endless sunshine, that eviscerating glare of white that bleaches the landscape and tans its residents into cancer and wipes away all shadows. The city lives by projecting light through shadows on film, but for the people in the industry, let no shadow ever be admitted. Let there only be light. In Los Angeles, that is where God's commandments stopped.

We are all sunbeams, we all radiate excitement about the future, we all have projects moving forward. The project. The treasured project. Even people on the periphery of the industry—the guy who makes his living doing computer repair—as he removes viruses from your computer, he, too, meanders into a tale of his project with Madonna and how things were really starting to catch fire because it was her "passion project."

The term "passion project" was new to me twenty years ago. How could you identify script A as a passion project and script B as somehow just a project without the passion? For a playwright, where there is never any certainty of monetary reward, every project is fueled by passion. But in Hollywood, the passion project comes from bitter writers and directors who wrote on assignment, nameless cogs in the immense wheel of production, who then turned to intensely personal projects as a way to maintain their artistic bona fides. The passion project was the script a writer labored on after studio hours, on his or her own time, motivated by nothing more than the desire to say something—and also presumably by ego.

Defenders of the passion project can point to auteur cinema figures throughout the twentieth century who insisted on following a personal artistic vision: Charlie Chaplin, Orson Welles, indie filmmakers of the 1970s—there's a long list. This is the gold ring they reach toward: the passion project that will somehow magically allow them to express themselves fully and also earn them the embrace of Hollywood. Once again, it is the gold-rush mentality, the resolute belief in the god of success and banishment of the shadow of failure.

Which is not to say that failure does not exist in Hollywood. It is real, and it sends writers and directors and actors to the bottom of a black pool without leaving a ripple.

I have been there.

Failure

Wearing a suit is the surest sign of abject failure for a Hollywood writer. Successful writers dress like high-school students from the 1970s: T-shirts, blue jeans, tennis shoes, a visual assault on The Man of our imaginations. "I don't have to wear a uniform (other than the one I'm wearing); I'm a creative artist and blue jeans are required for my art, like Jackson Pollock, except without the paint splatters."

The people in the industry who wear suits are on the business side—the agents, mostly (a tradition resuscitated by CAA during the 1980s and '90s, reintroducing the power suit concept to a city of open collars), and some of the studio executives who deal with accounting and advertising. Hollywood writers have doubled down on casual appearance, although interestingly enough there is still a distinct look that differentiates a grip from a writer: the grip will always wear cargo shorts. Writers disdain displaying their pale white calves.

But the fashion statement is about comfort. The industry writer's comfort is her highest priority, which is why she lives in a large house with a Guatemalan maid, and spends Christmas in Hawaii, and travels to Sedona over the hiatus in a desperate attempt to lose ten pounds amidst pampered luxury massages and hikes through the desert, and shops at Whole Foods, and generally morphs the pressure of writing for television into a wonderful excuse for self-indulgence. And make no mistake, there are pressures: notes from the studio, notes from the network, suggestions from the star, nudges from the production manager, bitching from the editor, muffled derision from the PAs. Every day, each creative step one makes is examined under a microscope and then critiqued—although the writer never knows if the critique is truthful, because it is always safer to be effusive to a person who might end up running a show and taking you along with her on the money train. But writers do get to show up for work looking like third-graders.

Woe be the writer who walks down Ventura Boulevard wearing a suit. It is the black spot handed you at the Men's Wearhouse, a scarlet F for Failure emblazoned across your entire body. A suit cannot mean anything except this once-proud writer who wore flip-flops to network meetings—who confidently strolled through the rows of cubicles outside a network executive's office, sniffing at the minions who were forced to at least don a collared shirt and closed-toe shoes to appear at CBS—now that writer must put on the suit of shame and tie the hangman's noose of a necktie in a Windsor knot, and report to an office somewhere. It is every writer's nightmare to find himself at age fifty in a blazer and Dockers slacks, knocking on the door of corporate America. The abrupt slide down into the abyss of loserdom can be triggered by a solitary failure, by losing the one job that keeps you in a T-shirt.

I have been fired from a writing staff, an experience shared by hundreds of successful writers, many of whom laugh it off or blame the executioner: "They were completely clueless, fucked up beyond belief." But for me, being fired was a soul-searing experience, an event that shook my confidence to the roots and echoes in my head a decade later. Even though the show I was dismissed from was a programmer, a routine television drama, I failed to pass Ben Johnson's basic writer's dictum: "I despise the man who cannot write to measure."

The setting for this nightmare was Universal Studios, and the show was named *Providence*. I had just spent four years writing for *Touched by an Angel*, which prepared one for virtually nothing else in Hollywood. It was a big success, a Top Ten show, anchoring CBS's Sunday nights for several years, and yet, rather than a springboard for its writing staff, it has proved more of an albatross.

Providence

Writing for a cop show gives one bona fides for writing cop shows; likewise, a law show or a medical show serves as a gateway to all those other medical and law shows on television. There are not a lot of angel shows. One might argue that other television dramas deal with human emotion, and branch off from a similar limb of exploring social issues and examining people in crisis. Yes, that is true, but a crucial difference is that the heroes of *Touched* never changed or grew as characters. They were angels, fixed in who they were, and so on that level it was hard for studio executives to imagine a show that was a soul mate.

Providence should have been that soul mate, or at least a transition to the world of soapy family drama. I should have been able to write for it. I have a family. I know families. *Providence* was a hybrid medical show. The lead was a doctor and her father a veterinarian. While I had never written for a medical show, I had written medical episodes for *Touched*. Once I spent an entire day watching autopsies at the Los Angeles morgue so I could properly write an autopsy episode. I still can picture the skull flap sliced open and pulled back to reveal the brain. Following the removal of brain tissue for examination, the flap is then placed back on top of the skull, as if someone reapplied the lid to a tin of Spam.

But apparently I could not write *Providence*. At least, I could not write it to the satisfaction of Bob DiLaurentis, the show runner. Hollywood show runners are the closest thing the modern age will ever know of what it was once like to run a medieval duchy. Within a TV show's credits, you may see several different people listed as executive producer. Some gain that title because they have deals with a studio and have provided the conduit to getting a show on the air; others because they have climbed up the ladder of writing, and no matter what their actual function on a program, will never take a lesser title. Often, the creator of a show is listed as executive producer even after that person has departed to other projects—but typically, only one person is the executive producer who is the show runner.

The effective television show runner combines a unique set of skills, foremost of which is writing, but they also include creating a vision for the dramatic arc of a season (how a show should play out and develop over thirteen or twenty-two episodes or more); being the final arbiter for the look of a show (the colors it favors, how it is cut, and so on); dealing with the show's stars (a political, psychological, and artistic job in and of itself); supervising editing; supervising casting; managing other writers; managing the budget of a program; dealing with the politics of keeping a network and studio happy; ensuring the production runs smoothly at the crew level; and odds and ends such as selecting Christmas gifts for the crew and passing judgment on craft services.

A network places millions and millions of dollars into the hands of a show runner, so the pressures are very high and the rewards can be fleeting. Superb show runners have my utmost admiration, and I have worked most recently with Jeff Melvoin (on *Army Wives*), who is the exemplar par excellence (and teaches workshops on the subject for the Writers Guild). Bob DeLaurentis was a cordial and effective show runner, which makes my failure more acute.

I first met Bob on an afternoon in April or May. *Providence* was looking for an upper-level writer. My agent sent some scripts over and Bob liked them, and we met in his office in Santa Monica. *Providence* had two sets of offices, one at Universal Studios and one in Santa Monica. The Santa Monica offices (set up, I believe, for the convenience of Bob and the creator of the show, John Masius, as they both lived nearby) were pleasant and could have been Coffee Bean & Tea Leaf headquarters.

Many television writing offices are off the lot these days, which is a shame. There is a thrill when one drives into a studio as a working writer. That little surge of energy has never dissipated for me, which probably speaks to the fact that I grew up in Columbia, Missouri, reading about Hollywood in its golden age and dreaming of the magic of a film studio. One of the sobering disappointments of actually working in television was discovering that with the exception of Paramount Studios' vintage writers' warrens, writers' offices no longer have the romantic look of *Sunset Boulevard*. They are interchangeable with any cubicled office building, a vivid illustration of the corporate nature of television.

On the day I met Bob, I parked in the obligatory underground parking garage, which is often the only public entrance to an office building in Los Angeles. When I first moved here, I had many baffling expeditions in which I parked on the street near an office building and then wandered around trying to find the entrance. I finally figured out that the architect's assumption was that anyone coming to a building in Los Angeles would of course park in the underground lot and walk in that way.

There are often no entrances to large office complexes on the west side of Los Angeles except through a parking garage, and the thin amenities of a valet: a Latino man wearing a white shirt, black vest, and black tie. (No T-shirt and flip-flops for these men who sprint through parking garages or dash across thoroughfares at night in front of a restaurant to get your car from a place on the street where you could have parked it yourself, had you had their energy and expert understanding of local parking regulations. No, these guys have to run in a vest and tie, because it is only the underlings in this town who must dress up.)

Parking garage entrances usually feature a slice of red carpet laid down in front of an elevator door, with a guy standing behind a little podium, a box on the wall behind him littered with keys hung on hooks. This is the Los Angeles equivalent of the portico and doorman of a New York City apartment building. At the time of this meeting, I understood this protocol, down to the ritual of asking the receptionist in the production office for validation as one was leaving, often with the quip, "I need validation, at least my therapist thinks so." So I entered the Santa Monica office building through the parking garage.

I remember greeting Bob, sitting on a couch, and feeling very confident. I had watched several *Providence* episodes and read several scripts—the usual cram job before an interview that pops up suddenly on your radar. Often a writer will get a call from his agent saying that "show X is hiring and they'd like to meet with you in three days," and you respond, "Yes, of course, I love that show," and then furiously learn as much as you can about it.

Bob was bald, concise, direct, clear-headed. He was a veteran show runner. He was the show runner, but the creator of the show, John Masius, was also still very much involved, particularly in editing, which was his passion. Through a strange coincidence, Masius had also created *Touched by an Angel*.

Masius (for some reason everyone called him Masius, not John) began his career on *St. Elsewhere*, which spawned an entire generation of television creators and show runners, including Josh Brand and John Falsey, Tom Fontana, and Mark Tinker, among others. Masius's own experience with *Touched* was truncated. CBS research in the early 1990s showed that America was interested in angels, so the network decided to create a show about angels. They hired Masius to do so. This choice in retrospect seems absurd: the earnestness of *Touched*, which helped make it a hit, is at odds with Masius's contrarian view toward faith.

Masius's pilot featured Roma Downey and Della Reese as angels who were more in the tradition of *Angels with Dirty Faces*, the angels of the 1930s and 1940s, a staple of light comedic films and plays. Cary Grant helps a bishop with his problems in *The Bishop's Wife*; in *It's a Wonderful Life*, the bumbling angel Clarence earns his wings with very little awe in his attitude toward his job; an angel named Michael in *Heaven Only Knows* sets the Book of Life straight about a Montana tough guy. There was a consistent approach to angels; they were recycled human beings, part of a worldview that placed angels just above the jovial quality of Santa Claus—beloved mythic figures best honored with a wink. Perhaps a feeling of security in the fixed role of religion made Americans comfortable with kidding around about angels.

After the existential horrors of World War II, acknowledging the existence of angels seemed absurd and trivializing them silly, so we dropped the subject altogether. But by the mid-1990s, a religious revival carried clout in America and business, so to portray angels as Masius did in his pilot—as irreverent wisecrackers—seemed both a throwback to Frank Capra's angels and a slap in the face to the core audience of believers. Masius's script carried many features of the show that would continue—Roma and Della helping people out of crisis, along with an Angel of Death—but it sounded off-franchise.

CBS asked for a rewrite. Masius refused. He was fired, or he quit. Whichever it was, he had nothing more to do with the show—except to collect payments as creator for each episode that aired. For the first two years of production, he was the most highly paid writer on the show.

When I met Bob, he was naturally interested in how *Touched* was going, what the experience was like, and I was pretty honest. Every TV show has its own dynamic—all happy TV shows are the same; every unhappy TV show is unhappy in its own way—and *Touched* was a unique mixture of happiness and chaos, in part because its unexpected success always seemed to have us behind the production eight ball.

As I sat down with Bob to interview for *Providence*, *Touched by an Angel* was at the apex of its popularity. It was an earnest show about angels working miracles in people's lives, and that made it very uncool in the conventional Hollywood world. It was no secret that the head of CBS did not care for the show; tough crime pieces were more his cup of tea, and the chagrin he experienced at having his Number One program feature angels telling weeping people each week that God loved them was something he found hard to abide. That attitude pervaded the industry—"Yes, it's a hit, but it's not a cool hit"—and all the writers were tarred by that brush.

When I was hired, Bob told me he was going on vacation and we'd get to work when the writing staff gathered for the new season. Looking back (one looks back at failure so many more times than one examines success), I wish I had insisted on an opportunity to sit down with Bob and spend an afternoon—several afternoons—discussing how he saw the characters, what story arcs he imagined for the coming season, how he liked to run the show. But I felt good, confident, filled with hubris. Bob introduced me to Tim Kring. On one level, Bob was hiring someone to eventually fill Tim's role on the show, which was co-ex (co-executive producer), the second in command.

When one watches the credits crawl of a television show (if anyone outside of the parents of people who work on those shows actually looks at those things), one sees a number of people listed as "producer." To a civilian, there must seem to be a lot of producers working on each television show—a co-producer, a producer straight up, a co-executive producer, and executive producers (often many of these). It must seem as though every television show is burdened with many people who call themselves producers, and what the hell does a producer do, anyway?

In the world of television—not film, just television—most of those producers are writers. There is a specific ladder of credits which writers climb as they advance in their careers: staff writer, story editor, co-producer, producer, supervising producer, co-executive producer, executive producer. The jump between story editor and co-producer signifies that now the writer theoretically also begins to engage in producing work: thinking about budget, having input in casting decisions and hiring decisions, weighing in with comments about locations and sets, and so on. I say theoretically because, as seems to be endemic in the television industry, each show has its own peculiarities, often determined by the show runner.

Bob returned from vacation and the staff met at the Santa Monica offices. It was the usual mix of a writers' room, with a few amiable veterans, a couple of nervous newcomers, and a couple of people in the middle who carried the angry intensity of those who have been put through the mill for a few years, realized they are every bit as good as those at the top, but aren't there yet. Television writers have almost no pedigree except that they have written television scripts.

We talked about character arcs through the season and ideas for individual episodes. I was fairly quiet, trying to gauge the gestalt of the show. I do recall, vaguely, with the blurred contours of a remembered nightmare, pitching a story idea early on and seeing in Bob's eyes a sudden wariness. My pitch was not the right tone, and it felt melodramatic to him; this show was not about big plot twists (which I'd been accustomed to at *Touched by an Angel*), but rather continuing interpersonal interrelationships, moving characters through emotional thrusts and parries week after week. I was used to writing what amounted to one-act plays. This was serialized drama.

I felt the floor fall out beneath me. I was losing the most essential feeling for a Hollywood writer: confidence. Confidence, that code word for immortality. Writers like to believe our words will live after us; that we will be among the Ascended Masters, existing on a spiritual plane in some psychic pad on Sunset Boulevard, with a full cocktail bar and four-hour work days throughout eternity. With particular horror, I remember a discussion about the episode in which the female lead would finally sleep with her new boyfriend. I chirped up, saying of course this was a big event and we'd want to make a full meal out of this. A young woman staff writer stared at me across the table and said, "It's not that big a deal." Bob agreed with her, and I felt like a Victorian relic who had somehow survived World War I and was adrift in the Jazz Age, bewildered by a set of basic assumptions of human behavior that simply no longer held true.

Masius ambled in occasionally. I quickly caught on that the moment he entered the writers' room, discussion pivoted to restaurants or sports. Anything to avoid what we were working on. Masius, it seemed, had ideas that were either great or terrible, and because he was the creator and executive producer, attention must be paid. It had apparently been decided long ago it was a better use of time to deflect his pitches before they could be launched. For someone who had a huge career and had created more than one hit show, when Masius did pitch, it was with an extraordinary and charming modesty. He lowered his head and always began with something like an invocation: "I don't know—I mean, fuck—this is probably a fucking terrible idea, but I was like, fucking thinking ... maybe somebody brings in a water buffalo ..." Then he would look away and chuckle.

It would be like that—an arresting, big idea, sometimes brilliant, sometimes awful. Masius was the beloved but drunken Irish uncle in a James Joyce story—part of the life of this household, clung to like grim death even with all of his flaws. And I felt like the tourist walking into the house, who was being politely tolerated until I left. There was never an embrace, because in a writing room that embrace occurs only after one has proven himself indispensable—through a great script. All manners of oddities and personality defects may be erased and then endured following a great script. A great script, however, is also a highly subjective matter. Writing that suits one show doesn't necessarily work for another. I read *Providence* scripts, trying to find their sweet spot. The scripts seemed fairly straightforward, but until one writes something, one never really knows the voice of a show from the inside out.

Probably as a defense mechanism against trauma, I have forgotten the plot of the first *Providence* episode I wrote. I remember a couple of essential facts: after I had finished the outline, which centered on a teenage boy, Bob asked me to change that character to a girl. I agreed immediately. This happens all the time in television writing, and I've gotten used to it over the years. "Let's flip it—it's the wife who had the affair and the husband is alcoholic." "Let's make the Steinbergs black instead of white." "It's the boy who is thrown from the car, not the driver."

These kinds of shifts sometimes occur for casting opportunities—"We can get James Earl Jones"—or more often because it's a way to take a story that is meandering toward the commonplace and give it a twist. The twist is something that drives network television as much as character. My problem is that I am a character-driven writer. Plot is my weak suit, engaging characters my strength. But in television, one must be flexible, if not malleable, and so I switched the teenage boy to a teenage girl.

However, I knew no teenage girls. I have two sons. Bob was the one with daughters. One can do research into specific character questions—how does an ER doctor handle a tracheotomy? How would a con man pull the wool over an elderly mark's eyes? What's the lingo of a real estate salesman? The more generalized notion of getting into the head and language of a teenage girl is tough. Especially when one has about two weeks to do it and make it come alive in a script.

I did my best. I wrote a draft, the feeling of flop sweat gathering under my arms. I felt unable to confide in my fellow writers. The young woman who had scorned my pitch about first-time sex clearly held me in contempt. I couldn't consult above my pay grade; to let Bob or the amiable and generous Tim Kring know I was nervous would be a bad sign. I felt comfortable with two writers, the talented and funny Carol Barbee and Rob Fresco, a staff writer who had been working in various capacities in film for years. But these were the people that, in a perfect world, I was supposed to supervise when Tim moved to his own show.

I was alone. I wrote, I pondered, I rewrote. I second-guessed myself. I rewrote again, and then again. But on the due date, I had to turn in the script. Now, a dozen years later, I turn over the pages of that script and cringe. I had overthought it. It was too cute, overwritten, not simple. Back then, I was in the bubble of belief that occurs whenever one finishes a script. You always believe something is good, otherwise you wouldn't turn it in.

I waited for a response. A day, then two days of radio silence from Bob. Silence is almost never good. If somebody loves something, they usually tell you right away. If they hate it, they have to consult others to determine the material is worthy of their hatred, then ponder what to do, how to fix it—all while the writer lives in a bubble of frantic hope.

Bob burst the bubble. He called me in and started with the worst words a writer can hear: "There are some good things in this, but …" The moment a writer hears that, he knows his script is a steaming pile of dog shit, about to be plucked from the Earth, encased in a plastic bag, and hurled into a dumpster. Bob said he simply didn't buy the teenage girl. It just didn't ring true. I couldn't argue.

He singled out one particular scene that he felt illustrated my lack of getting the show. It was a conversation between two characters following not-so-great sex. To write it, I thought about postcoital experiences, imagined the many unspoken things that hover in the air between two mismatched lovers, and wrote a scene I thought carried a lot of subtext. It wasn't Pinter, but it did leave much unsaid:

Bert and Joanie are in bed. Staring at the ceiling. Disappointed.

JOANIE: Hey.

BERT: Hey.

JOANIE: You okay?

BERT: Sure.

A beat.

JOANIE: You know, it's a process.

BERT: Right.

JOANIE: One time doesn't mean anything.

BERT: (half-heartedly) Yeah.

JOANIE: It's only in romance novels that there's fireworks and … whatever.

BERT: Sure.

A beat.

JOANIE: Can you hug me?

Bob said, "It's just not our show," and he rewrote the scene and indeed the entire script. Bob's revision told me that here was a show that lived on the characters articulating precisely how they feel and what their issues are and laying it all out for the audience. This was not a drama of unexpressed yearning. For network television at that point and for this show, all yearning must be expressed.

Now I had laid an egg. The mark of death was upon my office door. Once a writer has turned in a turkey, there's really no going back. Your reputation is made. The angel of death had smeared the red lamb's blood across my nameplate, sparing the junior writers who cautiously avoided me—a dead man walking.

Production began. We filmed at Universal, and there was a flare of excitement as I pulled into Jimmy Stewart drive and parked in the big concrete structure. I belonged on the lot. I was on the inside, one of the monkeys in the zoo watching the tourists glide by in their gondolas. The offices were the corporate steel-and-glass variety that has taken most of the charm and sense of place away from Hollywood writers. But there was the soundstage, and I was dispatched to work with our star, who had the peculiar habit of poring over scripts, reading closely and arguing vociferously over individual word choices—and then getting on the set and paraphrasing like crazy.

The father/veterinarian on the show was played by Mike Farrell, a brilliant and good man devoted to social justice, and I enjoyed talking with him. I would return from the set to our offices and greet the receptionist, who was a cheerful young woman, rail-thin, with wispy blonde hair. She was a friend of Bob's daughter and grew up in the industry. She was bright and sunny, and of course I was as charming and pleasant as I could be, because here was the most direct link to the inner life of the Duke. She was like the butler in a Noël Coward play, whose lowly position belies the fact that she knows more than anyone in the house.

I would then walk into Tim Kring's office and often found him playing his guitar and singing with Rob Frescoe. My heart sank. In high school, I was a nerd, or at least enough of a nerd—speech and debate, school plays, student government—that I was divorced from the popular culture of my day. I distinctly remember sitting in my bedroom (a basement lair, with a floor of concrete, bitterly cold in the winter, but mine) and listening to KTGR, the Top 40 radio station in Columbia. It was my link to popular culture. It was only in ninth grade that I bought my first record, the Beatles' White Album, and I think I graduated from high school owning about four LPs and a Woody Allen comedy album. I grew up in a college town, and my cool associates from high school went to Grateful Dead concerts and listened to the Band and had their own garage bands, and this music was woven into their lives.

Now here was Tim singing effortlessly, playing some tune of the 1980s that was apparently so universally known that Rob wandered in with his guitar and they started in as a duet and I was as out of place as a half-dickey at Altamont.

But I had a second chance. My contract called for me to write two scripts. Perhaps, miraculously, I would redeem myself. It was a gun violence story, and once again, I went to work. This time I abandoned my dignity and showed pages to Carol Barbee and Rob. I was fighting for my survival, so who cared if it was humiliating to appeal to younger writers for approval? Carol liked the script and I was ecstatic. I had pulled it off.

I turned in the script. Silence. Once again, a day went by, two days. I couldn't sleep. I had to continue coming to the office, but now a pall settled around me. Had I managed to blow it again? Then a call came. "Please meet Bob in his office." I walked downstairs and greeted the receptionist/friend of Bob's daughter. She looked at me as if seeing a ghost and then recovered and faked a thin smile.

I entered the room. Bob was there, along with Tim, and the house director, a co-executive producer. There was a sense of walking into a formal judicial hearing. Bob got right to the point: "There are some good things in here. Really good things." This was a variation on the classic theme, but Bob seemed to actually mean it. "The dog trainer—I put more check marks by those lines than I have all year." Check marks are good things; they note a laugh or a particularly good line. "But I don't think you get the show. Didn't you read our scripts?" "Yes, of course, I did. Okay, well, I'll go back in and rewrite—" Bob cut me off. "No, we'll do it. I don't think that would be productive. I don't know exactly what to do. But we'll do the rewrite."

I left the office. I walked past the receptionist and didn't look at her. I got in my car and drove home. The next day, I got a call from Bob. I was sitting downstairs in a little office we have at home. It has been carved out of a garage, with a cement floor—not unlike my old high-school bedroom. "Ken, this just isn't working. We're going to let you go. I'm sorry. You have a great work ethic. There were some really good things in your script. But it's just not working." I hung up the phone. I sat for a long time. I had never been fired. I didn't want to do anything, so I sat. I was now officially on the outside. An assistant would pack up my things and deliver them in a box to my house. I was at least spared that.

Tim Kring went on to create hit shows like *Heroes* and *Touch*. Carol Barbee worked with him on those, created her own show, and is a show runner herself.

Had I worked out at *Providence*, had I been somehow right, I could have hitched my wagon to those talented people. I could have had a mentor, or at least a comrade who somehow thinks my talent is worthy, and I would have integrated myself into the great machinery of network television, with its joys and headaches, but above all, with its sense of belonging to a tribe. Instead, I was outcast.

I returned to *Touched by an Angel*, at a reduced time commitment and salary as a consultant. I felt like a man out of time. I had tasted the bitter grapes of failure. I could no longer pretend that success was an aura surrounding me and glowing like an overexposed shot of film. I was exiled from Krotona. The only response could be to bury this episode of death deeply. Until now, when I unearth it as a piece of history, a shard of a script that tells a forgotten story.

Judy Garland and Mickey Rooney on the set of The Judy Garland Show, *1963.*

The Judy Garland Show

GEORGE SCHLATTER sits in the Hollywood Vault, gazing at a photograph. "There she is." The admiration carries a tone of urgency, as if a kinetic memory of energy moves him. The photograph was taken over fifty years ago on the set of the first broadcast of *The Judy Garland Show*. George produced that show. He was still a very young man. He had come to California to play football for Pepperdine University, was startled when he learned that this also meant attending classes, and took a theater class. He got the bug, and after almost graduating, he landed in Las Vegas, booking talent into clubs.

He remembers booking Ronald Reagan and a monkey into a Vegas club—they were the same act, Reagan cashing in on his *Bedtime for Bonzo* fame. Half a century later, after a lifetime of creating iconic shows like *Laugh-In* and *Real People*, Schlatter studies the Leigh Wiener photograph of Judy Garland and Mickey Rooney as if still mesmerized.

Judy sits with Mickey Rooney, her costar on the first episode (which ultimately was broadcast as episode number seven on air). They are serious, gazing off to their right, and seem to be completely alone. As with many of his photographs, Leigh Wiener captures depths of melancholy and nostalgia; we can't help but think of the two of them as teenage MGM stars and know the tortuous journey they had traveled in the twenty years since *Andy Hardy* and *The Wizard of Oz*.

On his television program *Talk About Pictures*, Wiener recalls the circumstance of the photo George Schlatter examines. He remembers he got the assignment to shoot the first broadcast performance of Garland's new variety show for CBS. After some debate as to whether to simply air the show live—1962 was just around the corner from the era of live television as the default choice—CBS decided to tape it in front of a live audience.

Wiener had been on the set for hours as they set up the broadcast and did sound

Judy Garland and Mickey Rooney in a publicity shot for the film Love Finds Andy Hardy, *1938.*

checks. He remembers that just as the show was beginning, a camera dollied toward the stage and a cable broke. Everything had to stop while the crew repaired the cable. Judy Garland was terribly nervous and Mickey Rooney seized a headset, reshaped his hair into two spiky points, and proceeded to improvise for the audience as though he were a Martian landing on Earth. It was funny, he filled forty minutes, and most importantly, he calmed Judy Garland down.

At one point during all of this turmoil, Leigh approached Garland and Rooney and asked to take their picture. Garland hesitated, but Rooney said, "Let's do it. He's been working all day. Let's do it right now." Leigh asked them to sit right where they were—on the side of the stage—and his one request was that they be serious.

In Wiener's eyes, Rooney was acting serious, but Garland was instantly and deeply serious to the bone. They appear to be completely alone in the photograph, but the reality was they were surrounded by stagehands, a crew, and an audience.

These two grew up on sound stages and performing, and perhaps a stage was as comfortable a place as they knew to become private and intimate.

George Schlatter remembers the first time he met Judy Garland:

> It was 1963. I had just gotten the job of producing *The Judy Garland Show*, and I was in New York for pre-production. I go into Mike Dann's office and in walks Judy Garland. I wasn't prepared to meet her, so I just blurted out, "I don't care what you may have heard, there's no truth to the rumor that I'm difficult!"

She burst out laughing and they left the CBS offices, had a drink, and remained close friends for the rest of her life. Schlatter always made her laugh, which was her natural default position in life. Liza Minnelli and all those closest to her remember Garland's essence as joyful, with a sharp wit and sense of humor that would cut through any crisis. George recalls creating a sound tape that was a sort of highlight reel of farts. Loud, long, toots, rips; it was a symphony of flatulence. Judy was onstage rehearsing, and at a moment when things got tense, George cued the fart tape over the loudspeakers. Garland collapsed in laughter.

Schlatter rigged an enormous trailer to be her dressing room, and he painted a yellow brick road that led from it to the stage. She loved the trailer and it became a home away from home. It was carpeted and contained a kitchen, a bar, and an office, along with her makeup room. A red-and-white striped canvas awning fronted the trailer, along with artificial grass and trees. The sign on the trailer door said "The Legend." The refrigerator inside was stocked with Blue Nun.

George remembers a moment when Garland left the stage upset during rehearsal. As she walked toward the dressing room, he joined her and started to sing "Somewhere Over the Rainbow." Garland turned to him, shocked, and said, "What the hell are you doing?" "Well," he replied, "if you're going to produce, I'm going to sing." She chased him down the hall, pummeling him until both were breathless with laughter. (It might be noted that Garland was tiny, barely five feet tall, and having the previous year gone on a month-long diet of two cups of tea a day—nothing else, no food, no vitamins, just two cups of tea—she had slimmed down from 185 pounds to 100. Schlatter still had the build of a collegiate football player.)

Schlatter got the job in equal parts because he lobbied hard for it and because he had produced *The Dinah Shore Show*. CBS at the time was far and away the most successful television network, even though it was run by network president James

Judy Garland on the set of The Judy Garland Show, *1963. Photo by Leigh Wiener.*

Aubrey, "The Smiling Cobra," and his West Coast vice president Hunt Stromberg Jr., surely one of the most despicable human beings ever to soil Hunter Thompson's "plastic hallways of television." CBS executive Alan Courtney is quoted in *Rainbow's End,* Coyne Steven Sanders's excellent account of *The Judy Garland Show,* describing Hunt Stromberg thus:

> [A] really repulsive human being. He ran the West Coast with an iron hand. The destruction of [fellow CBS executive] Hubbell Robinson was one of the most awful things I'd ever seen—it was like watching a snake swallowing a bird.

CBS envisioned *The Judy Garland Show* as being akin to *The Dinah Shore Show*—folksy, down-home, casual—everything that Garland's showbiz supernova was not. George Schlatter viewed the program instead as a "weekly special." His aim was to make each week have the aura of a Judy Garland special. Taping was scheduled to begin in the summer.

The biggest question advertisers and the Hollywood community asked was, "Can Judy Garland handle the grind of weekly television?" Many assumed, knowing her recent history of cancelling performances because of health issues, that she'd burn out very quickly and the show would collapse. Once the series was announced, CBS asked Garland to come entertain at an affiliates dinner in New York, essentially to assure them that she was up to the job. On the plane from Los Angeles to New York, Schlatter and Garland got an idea, and when she walked out on the stage to entertain the affiliate owners who constituted on one level her ultimate employers, she sang:

Call me irresponsible,
Call me unreliable,
Throw in undependable, too.
Do my foolish alibis bore you?
Are you worried
I might not show up for you?
Call me unpredictable.
Say that I'm impractical.
Rainbows I'm inclined to pursue.
But it's undeniably true –
I'm irrevocably signed to you!

George Schlatter remembers that the place went crazy. She had won them over. Work on the show began that summer, and Garland upended expectations by showing up, working hard—everyone associated with the show remarked on her ability to learn music and dance numbers almost instantaneously—and graciously putting up with the burdens CBS placed upon her, such as sticking her with an uncomfortably cast second banana/comic relief actor in Jerry Van Dyke. Van Dyke's role was never clarified, and the writing staff for the show was not Schlatter's choice but CBS's. Van Dyke was given the horrifying task of doing his malapropism shtick with speeches like: "Good evening, jadies and lentlemen! This is Derry Van Jyke welcoming you to the Gudy Jarland Show! ... Steady, Jerry, baby. After all, what is it? Just another show. And ... Good evening, Germans and Ladlemen! Oh, boy!" Van Dyke was painfully aware of the limitations of the material he was given, and during his days on the show started drinking.

Schlatter and the writers came up with a musical segment that would end each show. "Born in a Trunk" would feature Garland alone on stage, with a prop theatrical trunk recalling her childhood of touring vaudeville, singing one of her signature songs. For her first show, she came up with the idea of singing "Old Man River." To her knowledge, no woman had ever sung the song, let alone a white woman. CBS objected, of course; they wanted her to close with "Over the Rainbow." But Schlatter prevailed, and one can see on YouTube the resulting performance.

It begins with Garland on the runway, giving a little bow to the applause of the audience, and then it seems as though we are suddenly seeing her offstage. There is a slightly nervous hand gesture, she seems deep in thought, she tugs her hair back and begins singing. These little gestures that seem like a fascinating anti-performance—as if we have caught her before the show really begins—are they instead the consummate acting job? Misleading the audience into believing that she is so distracted in thought she has lost track of our presence, and we are now privy to a private moment? It very well may be. The delivery of the song is marked with a deep understanding of each phrase; it is the story of the song that is carried clearly, with a touch of humor and then a kind of radiant attempt to overcome the hardships of life.

Forget that Judy Garland never lifted one bale of cotton in her life or toted one barge. The lyrics become a metaphor for anyone's hard work. And then when she gets to "I'm tired of living and scared of dying," we feel, whether through art or searing reality or some magical brew of the two, that this is why Judy Garland wanted to sing this song so desperately. It was that thought—the horrible conundrum of life that we see on her face in Leigh Wiener's photograph, the dilemma that informs all of our lives—that she grapples with nakedly in that moment. She holds the last note, soaring, for measure after measure, and the audience goes wild and she bows and the spell is broken as we again see a tiny little woman on a stage alone.

After six shows, CBS fired George Schlatter. They wanted the show to be more like *Dinah Shore*—more folksy. They brought in Norman Jewison. George told me that Jewison looked at the first six episodes and said, "This is great. Why do they want to change it?"

The Judy Garland Show lasted its entire season. She made it through twenty-six episodes; the final episodes, taped after Garland knew the show was being canceled, became concert shows, with Judy holding the stage for the entire hour. The last show was a tortured taping experience, with Garland breaking down and a faithful audience staying through an endless night as the taping lurched from song to song.

She sang the first song, "Here's to Us," which would be placed within the show near the end as a salute to her musicians and the audience. It was received with cheers and applause, and Garland burst into tears and ran off to her trailer. There she discovered an orchid plant sent by Hunt Stromberg Jr. A card was attached to the plant: "You were just great. Thanks a lot. You're through. Hunt Stromberg Jr."

Thomas Kinkade.

The Painter
of Light

WHEN WE OPENED THE CRATE and revealed a large painting in an ornate gold frame, my wife asked, "What are we going to do with this?" I gallantly offered to hang it in my office, a little rented room on Ventura Boulevard that no one ever visits. God knows my wife didn't want it in the house. It is titled *The Christmas Cottage*, and it was a personal gift from the "Painter of Light," Thomas Kinkade.

He is dead now, so the story may be told. I spoke with Thom less than a month before he passed away, presumably killed by an unintentionally lethal combination of liquor and pills. Thom was enthusiastic on the phone—he was always enthusiastic—and he had a great story he wanted to tell the world. He always had a great story to tell the world. And now he is dead, a man whose life seems far removed from Hollywood, but in the end, Hollywood and the Painter of Light were deeply connected.

I met Thomas Kinkade because of my dog. Owning a dog in Los Angeles is a sufficient substitute for not playing golf. I have often envied writers who speak of cutting deals on the golf course. Walking along a green fairway, bonding with a studio executive, the endlessly blue sky overhead—of course a pitch sounds good along the broad sweep of a par five, and this is your trusted golfing buddy, and enveloped in the smell of freshly-cut grass and whiskey and cigars, a movie deal seems like an old-school natural.

I used to play golf in Minnesota, where I became famous for slicing my shots and then crying out, "Ken, you asshole!" which was cathartic but wouldn't inspire a producer's confidence. If you are golfing with colleagues in the film and TV industry, they want to see someone who is calm, collected, who can roll with the punches on the back nine because this is how you will roll with the punches on a film schedule.

I have not played golf in Los Angeles, but I have owned a dog, an amiable Wheaten Terrier named Kirby, and he introduced me to a couple in my neighborhood who always walk a pack of small dogs. Michael and Arla Campus are among the rarest commodities in Hollywood, a couple married for over thirty years who are genuinely devoted to each other. We became dog friends.

Michael's career had taken several improbable turns. As a young Jewish New Yorker, he worked for CBS during an age when network television featured such highbrow entertainments as a half-hour special devoted to Vladimir Horowitz. Having succeeded in this kind of sophisticated entertainment, he was transferred to Hollywood, and his first assignment was, naturally enough, to direct a blaxploitation film. The genesis of the script had been inside a prison, where a convicted pimp wrote bits of dialogue on sheets of toilet paper and gave them to the prison barber, who smuggled them out and somehow got them to a Hollywood agent. The agent saw blaxploitation gold. He sold it to a studio, and the studio saw in Michael Campus a hip guy who could work well with a radical black community. Michael took on the assignment, and the film became the cult classic *The Mack*. He has memorable stories about making the film in Oakland and his negotiations with the Black Panthers and star Richard Pryor, but he's writing his own script about that saga.

The Thomas Kinkade period of my life began when I met Michael walking Kirby one fall day and he told me that through a happenstance meeting in Carmel, he had become friends with the Painter of Light. Thom was interested in getting into movies, creating a franchise similar to Tyler Perry's empire, and wanted to start with a Christmas film. Did I have any ideas for a story?

As it happened, I had become the in-house specialist for writing Christmas episodes on *Touched by an Angel*, and I had an idea involving an old artist-mentor passing along one final lesson to his pupil at Christmas. I wrote it up, emailed it to Michael, and he reported back that he liked it and Thom liked it. But could it be more specifically about Thom's life? He wanted the story to be autobiographical. Thom did, in fact, have a mentor, a retired Berkeley professor and painter who moved next door to the impoverished home where Thom grew up with a single mother in the little mining town of Placerville, California.

I got on the phone with Thom, transmuted his life story into the outlines of the story I had proposed, and at the beginning of December Michael and Thom pitched the idea to Lionsgate Films. Lionsgate had struck a gold mine with its series of Tyler Perry films and saw a similarity: both Kinkade and Perry had devoted followings already, and a ready audience to tap into. Thom, always a master salesman, worked with us on constructing a sales pitch. Here is how it began:

> Imagine that 15 million American homes have a TV in their living rooms—and the picture never changes. The content is provided by one man. And these millions of Americans treasure that picture and the man responsible for it. Sound impossible? It's happening today. Every morning, 10% of Americans wake up and see a Thomas Kinkade painting. His art is part of their day; he's there with them as they go to sleep, he's at the heart of their home. His appeal cuts across demographic lines, party lines, religious lines: Evangelicals love his art, but so do Catholics. He's painting a 9-11 memorial for the city of New York, but rural America holds him as one of their own. He is the official painter for the Elvis estate but the faith community embraces him, too. He's painting the farewell portrait of Yankee Stadium for George Steinbrenner, and his holiday calendar outsells all others. Thomas Kinkade is the present-day Norman Rockwell, associated with uplifting canvases filled with light,

No one would ever call Thom modest, but all of the above was true. He took great pride in being everyman's painter, and holding the title of "official painter for the Elvis estate" was a banner he flew with delight. Lionsgate envisioned Thom's massive group of followers turning up in theaters and said yes on the spot. In a remarkable turn of events—these things never happen this quickly—I was dispatched to write a first draft to be turned in at the beginning of January. The plan was to film in the spring and get it into theaters for that Christmas.

Thom was ecstatic; we all were. He took an active role in pitching ideas about the script. We had long conversations about his father, a pivotal role in the film, and his life. His father was a wild man, a drinker who left his wife and sons and was employed by a pizza parlor in a neighboring town. He showed up on the odd occasion driving a beat-up car, popped open the trunk, and proudly presented his sons with copies of *Playboy*. He kept talking about taking them on a trip to Mexico, a pipe dream that never materialized. He spun tales about women and drinking, he was a crazy, tortured soul—but Thom always insisted that his father was not an alcoholic. He simply enjoyed life.

In retrospect, Thom's tremendous material success was a shellac applied on top of his father's mold. His remarkable and persistent denial of his father's alcoholism was a canary in the mineshaft that Michael, Arla, and I noted, but we never imagined it ending in tragedy.

One day, as Thom and I talked about his personal history, he showed me a group of paintings that he kept carefully locked away. They were work from his shortened tenure as a student at Berkeley and were completely unlike the polished commercial paintings of lighthouses and cottages that the world knew him by. I recall dark images, some abstract, some in a sort of Ashcan realist school. They seemed startlingly original in comparison to the work that had made him famous. I saw in them a serious and talented artist. Thom dismissed them as youthful aberrations. He insisted he would never let the public see them. I felt he was embarrassed by them; not because they were bad, but because to him they looked derivative—as if imitating the style of Edward Hopper or Renoir was less acceptable than creating calendar art.

Following his truncated college career, Thom traveled down to Los Angeles, where he worked as an animator and then tried to start selling his paintings. He quickly learned the kind of painting that sold. And he painted more in that style. And he sold more, and he painted more, and there was a snowball effect—he had successfully created a brand before anyone referred to such things. Over the years, the brand became an empire, with a chain of stores across America retailing Thomas Kinkade paintings. Along the way, he developed a method of reproducing his paintings—essentially high-quality copies with individual touch-up strokes added—that allowed him to market them as originals in some fashion and price them more as an artist would price a series of original lithograph prints. He became a millionaire.

He invested—or rather, his company did, as Thom always shielded his personal assets from the corporate ones—in enormously expensive printing processes. The printing plants turned out exacting reproductions, which were touched up and signed. Thomas Kinkade Galleries sprouted up in shopping malls. Thom worked the circuit and sold paintings and calendars and coffee cups. The head of Teleflora once told me that their largest sale each year was the Thomas Kinkade painted vase at Valentine's Day.

Thom became an industry, based upon his trademark ability to paint light—cottage windows glowed with light; light glanced off shorelines; lighthouses beamed through the fog. He was the Painter of Light. He was also an avowed Christian, and part of his fan base was southern and evangelical. His romance with his wife,

Nanette, was part of the story. In each of his paintings, he would hide the letter N multiple times. It was his Hirschfeld salute to his wife, and his fans loved it.

Thom stretched his net wide. His sales pitch to Lionsgate, declaring himself the new Norman Rockwell—America's painter—was to a great degree accurate. He had ascended to the heights of commercial artistic success, and then evolving technology dealt him a blow.

Thom had based his company upon mass reproduction techniques. He was a painter, but his market was never the world of New York galleries or fine art. Those painters and critics and collectors despised him, and he reluctantly despised them in turn. I say reluctantly, because he knew good art from bad. Just as many Hollywood writers who produce B pictures are tasteful, well-educated women and men who love reading George Eliot on the weekend, Thom loved great painters and could talk at length about the techniques of van Gogh or Chagall or Jackson Pollock.

Thom considered himself a democratic artist, an artist for the people, who told visual stories that are uplifting and inspiring. He painted his lighthouses, and then reproduced them and made them available to the masses, so that every pipefitter in America could have a real Thomas Kinkade in his living room.

But then the copy machine got better. It became possible to reproduce poster art for a fraction of what that had cost only a short time before. Companies no longer needed massive printing presses, let alone high-end ones, to produce calendars and posters and artwork for sale. Thom and his company were caught holding old, expensive technology. The truth was, his company was in deep financial trouble—and that was before the recession of the late 2000s. In retrospect, that was probably his driving reason for turning toward Hollywood and attempting to cash in on his fan base through film.

We didn't realize that during the euphoric time when *Thomas Kinkade's Christmas Cottage* was being made. We dashed forward with production. It was going to be a low-budget film, but Michael wanted to get the finest actor he could for the role of the mentor. Who could be right for a brilliant artist near the end of his life? Peter O'Toole. An impossibly high target, but Michael sent the script to O'Toole's agent—and miraculously, an answer came back: Yes. Peter would like to do the film.

Rapid negotiations followed. Peter's quote was met—he would only have to work one week—and then the role of the mother was cast with the immensely talented Marcia Gay Harden. Suddenly this little movie, which might have felt like the filmic version of calendar art, had a pedigree. Lionsgate, a Canadian company,

The author with Peter O'Toole on the set of Thomas Kinkade's Christmas Cottage, *2007.*

chose to shoot in Vancouver, which was fine, as a million things are shot there and the city has a deep base of excellent local talent. The notes from the studio were not extensive; I was happy to do a rewrite. Michael and Arla gathered together first-rate designers and a crew. Incredibly, by late spring we found ourselves in Vancouver, in a production office, ready to start shooting. The biggest problem we faced was a verdant spring, and the film was supposed to take place at Christmastime. Never mind; Thom grew up in Placerville, California, and audiences would accept a green California Christmas.

The one concern we had was reports from halfway across the world. Peter O'Toole was in China shooting a television miniseries about the building of the Canadian railroad. (He played a businessman who went to China to conscript Chinese workers.) We got word that he was frail and unable to work more than four hours a day. This was troubling, as we were on a very tight schedule—twenty-six days to shoot the entire movie—and could not afford any delays. If Peter could only shoot half-days, well, that was a concern.

The entire time, all communication had been between Michael and Peter's agent. I completed the production rewrites—not really large—and we sent a final script off to Peter. A day or so later, Michael got a troubling email, and this was directly from Peter. It said that he had signed on to do the original script, which he loved and had committed to memory, and this was the script he wanted to do. Could a writer ask for a better email? Every draft we turn in, we believe in, and when Peter O'Toole says he loves your script and has memorized it, it seems like a little miracle.

Michael said, "Fine, let's change all of Peter's scenes back to the original," and so I did a sort of reverse-engineering draft in which all of those scenes reverted back to the way they had been, and then I had to make adjustments so that things tracked accordingly. Shooting began. The terrific young actor playing Thom, Jared Padalecki, was excellent, Marcia was wonderful and full of ideas, and we all nervously awaited the day Peter was scheduled to arrive.

Finally his plane landed, he was taken to the set (which was in a small town on the outskirts of Vancouver), and we got a call that he had arrived and was getting fitted for his costume. Michael and I walked down a little dirt road toward the costume trailer to meet him. We turned a corner and there he was, standing in the road, wearing just a T-shirt and chinos in the warm spring day, taller than I had imagined he would be, very thin and very Peter O'Toole. He greeted us cordially. He looked in my eyes, and then, as if reading my mind, put a hand on my shoulder and said, "It's going to be fine."

We went back to the set and concluded that day's work. The next morning, we were to shoot Peter's first scene, which was the penultimate moment in the film. It was a big set speech about the meaning of art, in which Peter walked into the back door of the little crappy house the Kinkade family lived in when Thom was growing up and gave a sort of summation about art's place in this young man's life. Marcia, who was thoroughly committed to the film, pointed out that this big speech could be framed by the Christmas tree in the background if Peter worked his way around the kitchen table. Michael and the cinematographer figured out the shot, and we were all set for the morning. The unanswered question was just how frail Peter actually was.

The next morning, he arrived from costume and makeup and we were ready for a first rehearsal. He said casually to Michael, "Why don't I just try this once?" and Michael said fine. Peter went out the door and Michael called action. Peter entered, planted himself, and delivered the speech word for word, with perfect passion and integrity and soaring emotion. The entire crew's jaws were on the floor.

Michael quickly said, "Let's shoot this," and began working. Peter delivered every take of the scene—both his side and coverage (when the camera was on Marcia)—perfectly and at full emotional strength. It was stunning, and he worked the entire day without pause. It was a dream come true for any writer—to have one of the world's greatest actors invested in your words—and what came out was that the rumors of his fragility were not in the least true. Apparently (and astoundingly) in China, the producers and crew didn't fully understand his stature and didn't even give him his own trailer. Peter is a longtime man of the people, but attention must be paid, and his response was to do the job, but just to the degree necessary.

Peter gallantly also took on a new scene, one which evolved from a thought Marcia had that there should be a scene between Thom's mother and his mentor—and also possibly because how could she resist not having a two-hander scene with Peter O'Toole? I wrote it quickly, and he memorized it and delivered it beautifully, even though he said that he was uncomfortable with this. I realized he was truly of the old British school, where one takes time with material, commits it to memory, and arrives to work with a fully realized character and performance.

One evening, he regaled us with stories about the filming of *Lawrence of Arabia*. He must have been dining out on these tales for fifty years, but the other side of the coin was also true: everyone wanted to hear what it had been like. My favorite story told of the company's complete isolation in the desert while they filmed. The only news they received of the outside world was through weekly deliveries of newspapers. He and Omar Sharif saw photographs in these papers of a new dance craze called "The Twist." Omar and Peter created their own version, constructing it from the photos in the papers, and dubbing it "The Cairo Shuffle." Peter got up and executed a few steps, and it looked every bit as entertaining as Chubby Checker's.

Thom was present for the beginning of filming and then left, returning toward the end. He makes a cameo appearance in the film. As the young Thom we see in the movie tells us that he has always remembered his mentor, we see Thom painting, putting the finishing touches on *The Christmas Cottage* painting (which was, of course, sold in Thomas Kinkade Galleries). Thom was engaged with the entire process, full of suggestions for the story, even suggesting dialogue, but always respectful of Michael and me. The filming ended on schedule, and everyone felt good about what we had done.

Michael went into editing, and I would periodically visit him in the edit facility on Ventura Boulevard. The film was scored and cut, and then a preview was arranged. I suppose there is something to be said for a random preview audience; one gets a sense of how a film plays in front of a haphazard collection of individuals taken from a suburban mall, and so there's some objectivity. But *Thomas Kinkade's Christmas Cottage* would never play well before mall rats or teenagers in general. I heard that the preview was okay, and the numbers were positive but not glowing. Fair enough.

Then in August, just at the moment when the marketing decisions were being made about how to promote the film, Lionsgate added a new, third member to their elite management team. Lionsgate had been struggling, and his job was to trim costs. He made a decision: *Thomas Kinkade's Christmas Cottage* would go directly to DVD. There would be no run in theaters. And, as it turned out, almost no marketing. Michael was heartbroken, but being a fighter, he organized a screening in Carmel for Kinkade fans. It came off beautifully, with the kind of response one hopes from a fan base, but Lionsgate was unmoved.

Years later, Michael told me a missing piece of this puzzle: Lionsgate had always assumed that Thom would invest his own money in the production, just as Tyler Perry had done in the early years. No one knew it at the time, but Thom had no money to invest. Lionsgate pulled the plug and now *Christmas Cottage* is consigned to screenings every Christmas on television, which is not a horrible fate, but it's not the fate the film deserved.

Nor did fate treat Thom himself kindly. After the film was consigned to the DVD sales rack (this was when Blockbuster still existed), I didn't hear from Thom. Michael gave me sporadic updates: Thom's company had bottomed out. The CEO, whom we always knew was the voice of sanity in that world, had left. Thom's marriage had broken up. He was involved with a lovely Iranian woman, who was his age and intelligent and interesting. She had a fascinating life story.

Then one day, out of the blue, I got a call from Thom. He was excited. His new girlfriend's story would make a great movie. He was coming back to Los Angeles. Could we get together for lunch? We needed to talk about pitching a movie based on her life.

Yes. One always says yes—who would have thought the earlier film would ever have seen the light of day? I said yes, let's get together, and then just a couple of weeks later, I learned from a headline online that Thom was dead. Michael called and told me what he knew, which was a sketch of Thom's last days. His new girlfriend had last seen Thom the evening of his death. He seemed fine, although he had returned to drinking and using drugs. He went up to his room; she left and then found him the next day. He had mixed liquor and pills and never woke up.

His divorce to Nanette was just a day from being finalized—but it was not final. So he died a married man. About a month later, there was an article in the *Los Angeles Times* about a bitter legal fight brewing between Nanette and the new girlfriend. Nanette has legal hold on Thom's property, even though Thom wrote a letter specifying certain assets he was giving to the new girlfriend. That remains unresolved at this writing.

An artist who finds what America wants and sells it to them, repeating himself time and again with only slight variation, as long as they keep buying: that is the Hollywood formula, and Thom executed it perfectly in the medium of oil painting. And like Hollywood, when the disruption of new technology upset the economic model, he was thrown for a loop.

Hollywood is massive enough and sprawling enough that it could right itself and make adjustments and remain profitable as an industry (even if the middle-class wage earners in that industry took a big hit, which we all have as studios endlessly trim production costs). Thom couldn't find an answer. Or he found it personally in drugs and drink, a time-honored custom for artists staring at the abyss. Would he have been better off had he pursued those student paintings he showed me one day? Would he have had the satisfaction of painting something more authentic to himself? Or were the lighthouses and cottages glowing with light really somehow an authentic expression of this man?

If one accepts that any work of art tells us something about the artist, then perhaps *The Christmas Cottage* speaks of Thom: enthusiastic, filled with good intentions, sentimental, conveying something true and something manufactured—and before I judge it, let me remember it must tell us something about me, too.

Micky Moore with Gloria Swanson in Cecil B. DeMille's Something to Think About, *1920.*

The Man Who Worked in Movies
for Eighty-Four Years

THE TITLE IS NEITHER A TYPO nor an exaggeration: Micky Moore literally worked in film from 1916–2000. He began his career as a child actor in silent movies, appearing with Mary Pickford, Tom Mix, and Gloria Swanson, cresting as a legitimate twelve-year-old star in Cecil B. DeMille's *The King of Kings*. Then, facing the conundrum of every child actor—growing up—he moved behind the camera and became one of Hollywood's greatest second-unit directors.

He directed his own films as well, helming Elvis Presley in *Paradise, Hawaiian Style* and Roy Orbison in *The Fastest Guitar Alive*, but within the industry, he was the acknowledged master of the second unit. He was responsible for the chase through the market in *Raiders of the Lost Ark* and much of what you see in *Patton*, and he did the second-unit work on *Butch Cassidy and The Sundance Kid*. He was still in demand when he was eighty-six years old and finished his career in 2000, directing the second unit of *102 Dalmatians*. His life spanned the history of American film—and what are the chances you have heard his name? Unless you work in the industry, slim.

I am standing on the deck of Micky Moore's beachfront home, which stretches in a V over a rocky piece of Malibu coast. A couple hundred feet up the shore is a very nice break in the surf, which is why he bought this property. His daughter Sandy remembers the day he came to look at it. Micky walked onto the back porch, saw the break in the surf, and said, "We'll take it." His wife plaintively asked, "Shouldn't we look at the house first?"

Hollywood Digs

Micky was, as both of his daughters attest, a man of action. He loved to surf, he loved to lead teams, and he loved to build things with his own hands, such as an addition to this home. Around the corner of the deck is an outdoor shower, with a backsplash of painted ceramic tile. The painting, done by his longtime script supervisor Jules Stewart (mother of actress Kristen Stewart), shows Micky on a surfboard, effortlessly riding the waves, and stenciled on the surfboard is a camera. In many ways, the image of someone serenely navigating choppy waters is an ideal metaphor for a second-unit director.

Second-unit directors are the unsung heroes of big movie shoots. When asked, "What is the role of the second-unit director?" Micky Moore answered, "The role of the second-unit director should be to never let the audience know what the second unit shot." While the first unit is shooting dialogue and close-up scenes with the lead actors, a second unit of crew shoots action sequences, using doubles for the stars. This saves time during production, and saving time means saving money. Time and money are really the only things producers have been known to kill for.

The best example of the kind of work a second-unit director does may be Micky's tour-de-force: the truck chase through the bazaar in *Raiders of the Lost Ark*. An early version of the script drew inspiration from director Steven Spielberg's 1971 TV film *Duel*, and the first storyboard laid out the truck chase on top of a mountain range. Micky pointed out that it would be hard to get the effect of a speeding truck when shooting it against a background without markers. He suggested placing the scene in a crowded area, and the sequence in the movie is a memorable chase through a bazaar.

Micky filmed that chase. It had to fit seamlessly into the style and tempo of Spielberg's vision, which brings up another essential quality for the job: selflessness. The second-unit director's job is to capture the tone and feel of the director. If successful, no one will ever give you credit for your artistic vision, because you have expressed the director's style, not your own. It requires someone who loves filming almost more than life itself, and Micky Moore was just that man.

Micky Moore's mother, Norah, turned her back on a well-to-do Dublin upbringing at the end of the nineteenth century to take to the London stage. Businessman Thomas William Sheffield saw her on stage when she was perhaps seventeen, fell in love, wooed her extravagantly—he bought out the theater for one performance—and wed her. Following business setbacks, Sheffield moved the family to Canada, and Micky was born in British Columbia in 1914. Shortly thereafter, the family moved again, this time to Santa Barbara, California, which was then one of America's nascent film centers.

Micky Moore with William Boyd in Cecil B. DeMille's The King of Kings, *1927.*

Santa Barbara was home to the American Film Manufacturing Company, its logo of an "A" against a backdrop of wings giving it the nickname "The Flying A." The Flying A specialized in Westerns and at the time was one of the largest studios in existence. (Today only a corner of the original lot remains, a white stucco building with arched windows on a Santa Barbara street.) Norah took Micky's older brother, Pat, to the studio when she heard they needed a four-year-old actor, and he landed the part. During filming, she brought eighteen-month-old Micky along to the set, and he ended up being cast in four Flying A productions. Norah used her own last name as a stage name for Micky, and his career had begun.

Sensing that bigger things were afoot, the family moved to Hollywood in 1916. Micky recalls their home on North Vine Street, lined with pepper trees. Silent film stars such as Theodore Roberts, Monte Blue, and Sessue Hayakawa were neighbors. Just down the street from their house, in a barn at 1521 Vine Street, Cecil B.

Micky Moore (center) at a birthday party with young actors on the set of The King of Kings, *1927.*

DeMille shot *The Squaw Man,* the first full-length feature film. Pat had a plum role in the film, and there is a photo of the two brothers with star Anne Little on the set.

Micky had a halo of curly blonde hair, and when he was very young played both boys and girls. Norah kept meticulous records of the family's engagements, and she recorded Micky's first big role, supporting Mary Pickford in *The Poor Little Rich Girl.* He appeared with Pickford again three years later in her hit film *Pollyanna.* The photo of the two together—both Irish, with ringlets of curly hair—makes their pairing as mother and son seem seamless. Micky was soon making $200 a week, four times the amount the average American laborer earned then, and he appeared with John Gilbert, Harry Carey, Jack Holt, Tom Mix, Gloria Swanson, and Tyrone Power, senior. If Tyrone Power Jr. seems like a bit of ancient history in 2013, how much more remarkable is it that someone who passed away this year acted with the man's father?

Playing Mark in DeMille's *The King of Kings* was the highlight of the decade for

Micky, not least because of the lasting impact DeMille would have on his life. The transition from silent movies to talkies in the late 1920s coincided with Micky's entering adolescence and the awkward years of casting. It was as if the entire film industry's voice changed, and there was a scramble for Hollywood's new identity. In 1929, at the age of fifteen, he acted in his last role, in *This Day and Age*, directed by DeMille. The stock market crashed in October, taking the family finances down with it. Within a year, Norah, Pat, and Micky were working at a grocery store.

This astounding reversal of fortune summed up the tragedy of the Great Depression. The world of silent movies crashed alongside the general economy and led to the sort of *Sunset Boulevard* pathos of great stars reduced suddenly to terribly mundane existences. In Micky's case, by 1933, he was working fishing boats off the Santa Monica pier, hauling passengers and getting up early to catch live bait for fishermen. (While working on the ocean, Micky learned to surf, taught by Duke Kahanamoku himself.) Micky decided he had to get back in films and got an appointment to see "Mr. DeMille," as he always refers to him in his autobiography.

DeMille assumed that Micky had come to him looking for work as an actor. To his surprise, Micky said that he wanted to work in the property department. Why props? When Micky worked on *The King of Kings* as a twelve-year-old, he became good friends with DeMille's assistant director, Roy Burns, and Bob McCrellis, his property man. Now Burns was production head and McCrellis was master property man on DeMille's current film, *Cleopatra*. Micky saw the world of props as a point of entry.

DeMille hired Micky, and he began working behind the camera. Property departments had grown up during the silent era, when they were tasked with nearly impossible feats. Scenarios of comedies often depended on having the right prop, or creating one on the spot. With the advent of talkies, the right prop was still vital—that remained a constant in the world of sound. Micky was first assigned to the swing gang, which works ahead of what's being shot. Then he became a second property man, which meant working with the first property man, who thought through the prop needs with the director. Micky had known filmmaking from the actor's point of view before he could talk; now he was learning the minutiae of planning shots, from the smallest physical object on up.

He worked his way up as property man during the decade of the thirties on films like *The Plainsmen*, *Souls at Sea*, and *Union Pacific*. He learned how to handle explosives on *The Buccaneer*, in which Fredric March played the pirate Jean Lafitte, and he spent weeks at a time on a three-masted schooner in the Channel

Islands filming *Rulers of the Sea*. In the 1940s he worked on thirty films, including doing props for two classic Preston Sturges films, *Hail the Conquering Hero* and *The Miracle of Morgan's Creek*. He was the master property man on everything from *Incendiary Blonde,* starring Arturo de Córdova and Betty Hutton, to the Hope and Crosby road film *Road to Rio*.

His daughters remember working as extras in the Bob Hope comedy *The Paleface*. Tricia says, "All the kids of anyone working at the studio would do extra work. It was just what you did." The studio system, for all its madness and manipulation of people's lives, felt like a small town from the inside. Paramount hired parents and then hired the kids. People's lives would cycle through the system; Micky worked as property man for Sam Wood, who had directed him as a child actor in the silents.

At the end of the decade, Micky was offered a step up, and he jumped at the opportunity: he became a second assistant director. In the finely calibrated world of film positions, the second assistant director is the person who takes a script and breaks it down. (This was true in the old studio system and is still true for big productions now; often in television there is only one assistant director.) Before computers, the second assistant director was charged with putting all of the crucial information about what was needed to shoot a scene on breakdown sheets, and then transferring that information to colored strips of paper. The strips (which identified the location of the scene, actors involved, script pages in the scene, and so on) were put into a scheduling board, which was a sort of master calendar. There is a certain romance to the old school strips of the breakdown board, lost now as everything happens digitally, including, frequently, the shooting itself.

Micky moved up to first assistant director on *When Worlds Collide*, a science-fiction film that won an Oscar for best special effects. Into the sixties, he continued to work as first AD on Jerry Lewis movies and three Elvis movies (*Blue Hawaii, Girls! Girls! Girls!* and *Fun in Acapulco*) before finally getting the chance to direct in 1966 with *Paradise, Hawaiian Style*. At that point, he had been working in movies for forty years. The bulk of his career was still ahead of him.

There is a kinetic appeal to film work. Despite all the standing around between shots, it is intensely physical. Immense sets are constructed; heavy and complex lights are hung; crews are moved like small armies; locations in extraordinary places have to be scouted and mastered. Reading Moore's autobiography, *My Magic Carpet of Film*, one is struck that here is someone who lived for getting the shot. Case in point, his commentary on the filming of his first movie. After forty

Micky Moore with Muriel McCormac in The King of Kings, *1927.*

years in the business, he was finally directing, but the bulk of what he writes about centers on achieving a helicopter shot in the narrow Waimea Canyon in Hawaii:

We were flying in James Gavin's Bell 47-J-2 helicopter with Gavin at the controls. Nelson Tyler, my aerial camera operator, was behind the camera that was mounted on a Tyler Mount. I was sitting directly behind Gavin looking into a small monitor which showed me what Tyler was filming as we raced toward an opening in the cliffs. During the shooting of this sequence, we had been blown back from the opening two times. It was during our third approach coming in from the ocean through the gorges of Waimea Canyon that we flew into the narrow opening at the top of the 2,000 foot Na Pali Cliffs. There are no words that can describe the view I saw in the monitor as we cleared the walls of the cliff and descended down through those cliffs into the canyon below. All I could think of was this same shot had to be duplicated! We needed the same angle only following the plane supposedly being piloted by Elvis. What we had just shot would be used as hit point of view [known as a POV shot],

What would possess someone to risk his life for the sake of a shot in a film that would be promoted as "Elvis—a Copter Flyboy with More Co-Pilots Than He Can Handle!" and "Elvis—Surrounded by the World's Most Wonderful Wahinis!"? Who gambles his life to capture a moment on film in a desultory B movie? The Hollywood professional. There is a code of honor among the real Hollywood professionals, an idealistic and silent pact with God to give everything one has to whatever film one is working on. Not unlike the soldier, who cannot choose whether he is fighting a noble war, a good war, a stupid war, or just going to battle, the filmmaker and the crew take on a mission, and the quest to fulfill that mission—whether it is capturing Elvis singing "House of Sand," surrounded by bikini-clad wahinis doing the Frug, or Citizen Kane murmuring "Rosebud"—is sacred.

Perhaps this explains why Micky embraced becoming a second-unit director. He could have held out for more directing jobs after his two films were moderate successes. But it was the work that was the gold ring. Getting into the arena with a piece of material and wrestling it to the ground—choreographing the chase in *Raiders of the Lost Ark*; creating the flying basketball sequence in the remake of *Flubber*, starring Robin Williams; re-creating battle sequences from the Second World War for *Patton*—was more exhilarating than waiting to be the man in charge of the entire movie.

At Micky Moore's home, his daughters have sorted out the many binders that Micky preserved from his films. Here is a binder full of storyboards from *Raiders of the Lost Ark*. A notebook is filled with production shots from *Paradise, Hawaiian Style*; Micky and Elvis and a film crew sprinkled among the long lines of cables and forest of lighting equipment that always ring a set. Here is a notebook with pictures from the Jerry Lewis and Dina Merrill comedy *Don't Give Up the Ship*, the complicated lines of electricity and lights set up on board a cruiser.

Here is a production photo from the 1959 blacklist film *Career*, co-written by Dalton Trumbo. It's a Greenwich Village street scene, with Dean Martin and another actor before a cheap clothing storefront displaying suits on the sidewalk. The street is dressed for winter with fake snow and extras in long coats, and a hot dog cart propped up on apple boxes to give it the right height. All that goes on in the

Micky Moore directing Suzanna Leigh and Elvis Presley in Paradise, Hawaiian Style, *1966.*

right side of the photo. On the left is the apparatus of filmmaking: a long boom mike, a camera, lights, grips standing and waiting to move the camera, Mickey on the scene behind the camera operator. For this one shot in a low-budget comedy, there is an enormous investment in crew, planning, set dressing, equipment, extras, signage—all for the briefest of moments on screen.

On back through time the notebooks go until we arrive at single sheets of contracts. There is a contract from Lasky Studio (Famous Players-Lasky Corporation) dating from 1921 engaging Mickey (sic) Moore for Production Number 328 to play the character of Boy.

Film is such a new medium that one man's life can virtually span its history. How long did it take for humanity to build the traditions of warfare, to establish codes of honor and the hierarchies of battle? Film has inspired that kind of loyalty, the unswerving dedication to a cause, within the blink of an eye. What is there about

Micky Moore with unidentified woman, late in his career.

movies that has made fanatics not only of audiences, but also those who work on making movies? I believe this might be a phenomenon that existed only for the moving pictures, and only during the twentieth century. Every other art form in human history—theater, dance, music, painting, sculpture—could also be the domain of the amateur. Anyone could write a play and gather friends together to read it or perform it on the back porch. Anyone could dance; anyone can play a guitar; even sculpture is available to the amateur for the price of some clay. But to make a movie in the twentieth century required an immense amount of money. (I quickly add that while home movies thrived during the past century, in no way could they be confused with commercial filmmaking. Steven Spielberg may have shot movies on Super 8 in high school, but no one watches those. The poems that a young Emily Dickinson wrote are still read because their art requires none of the infrastructure of film.)

Film—acetate film—cost money. It was expensive to light properly. Sound equipment was expensive. The crew to mount a film set, light it, rig it, and get the sound recording was expensive. Until the advent of digital cameras and the Internet—the twenty-first-century democratic revolution in filmmaking—film required a large investment, which could only be supplied by an organization like a film studio. So there was the sense of joining an elite cadre. If initially stage actors turned their noses up at this lower medium, within a relatively short period of time, the financial sway of movies pulled in the best actors, writers, and directors. To be part of a film set was like being a Green Beret: it was reserved for the few who could handle the extraordinary pressures and demands that filming requires. (Such as fourteen-hour days for weeks at a time, dealing with emergencies in foreign lands, handling the bizarre combination of the demands of stars and the demands of producers, and so on.)

This sense of pride and an unparalleled work ethic hoisted filmmakers like Micky Moore to the top of the profession. The best had a sense of teamwork that again mirrors the military. His daughter Tricia remembers that her father might say, "We need to dig this Jeep out of the sand immediately," but he would always be the first guy to pick up a shovel.

At the end of his autobiography, Micky lists questions he was frequently asked and his responses. To the query "What is the best time or best part of making a film?" he answers:

> It is always a great moment when you finish a film on time and on budget. But it's also great when you are able, as second unit director, to start a film project at the beginning of the process, giving your input and becoming a truly collaborative team. And, finally, it's a great feeling to see the final product when it is shown to audiences.

His answer incorporates the beginning, middle, and end of the filming process—but he starts in the middle, when the film is completed "on time and on budget." It is the glory of doing the job right that always appealed to Micky. He passed away in 2013, at the age of ninety-eight. The twentieth century, the century of film, was his century.

Farley Granger.

A Neighborhood
Walk

I AM SITTING in our home office, jury-rigged out of an old garage, and I am trapped by a film crew. We have rented our home out as a location to shoot a commercial. We do this every couple of years because the money is good, and after about two years one forgets the pain of being the homeowner on a set. For all the joys of working on a film crew—the sense of camaraderie; the schmoozing with the always delightful hair and makeup ladies; the chatter from wandering grips wearing cargo shorts and sunglasses perched atop their deeply tanned faces as they head to craft services with its intriguing assortment of junk food that one would never normally eat, but hey, it's a shoot; the intimate gossip about talent that goes on in "video village," with its array of directors' chairs full of people with jobs that apparently require them to watch video monitors of what is being shot—all these little joys, including the sense of belonging to a vast and ambitious project, are lost upon the homeowner.

The homeowner sits helplessly (if he is foolish enough to stick around during the shoot instead of handing the reins over to a location manager) and watches as a horde of crew, like a swarm of locusts, sweeps into the home, laying down cardboard and rolls of carpet over the floor, taping bumpers around every corner, lining the halls with more protective cardboard, and setting up power lines on the front porch and portable tents to shelter craft services. Immense lights are hauled off trucks, the homeowner's personal furniture is rapidly dispatched to the backyard, and the home you thought was yours is reduced to its bare material outlines, swathed in layers of carpet and cardboard like the padded cell of a madman. You suddenly realize what you live in is simply walls and a floor and everything else is interchangeable. It is fun to ride the pirate ship and sail the seas with a crew of amiable cutthroats; it is not so much fun to be the civilian on a sailboat being boarded.

Grips with colorful braided beards, and the art director in a very hip short dress, and her assistant, a strikingly beautiful mocha-skinned woman, and the director of the commercial, who is British (for some reason all commercial directors seem to be British), are now walking through what a few minutes ago was your living room but is being transformed into something else—something that is supposed to represent the abode of a young artsy type, and the set piece decorations are colorful but it never looks actually lived in—and it is time to flee this conquest of your home. And so I set off on a neighborhood walk.

Kitty-cornered from our house in Studio City is the large home of the actor George Wendt, and the house is like the actor: casual, embracing, and stout. It sits heavily on the corner, fenced in, and we can hear his son's garage band practicing and occasional parties from the backyard. I wander toward Laurel Canyon and pass the home of Ed Begley Jr., its roof festooned with solar heating panels, and the fence along the side made out of recycled milk cartons. Ed's electric car is usually parked outside, although he is often seen riding his bicycle through the neighborhood.

There are two kinds of celebrities in Los Angeles, one sometimes thinks: the invisible and the highly visible. George is, for the most part, invisible; it's rare to see him. Ed is more like the mayor of Studio City—a spokesman for the environment, involved at Carpenter School, hanging signs up on his fence for the neighborhood Fourth of July parade.

Two blocks up Laurel Canyon is a residence with a guesthouse in back that has been converted into a little soundstage. My friend R.J. shot Internet music pieces there, filming a spokeswoman against a green screen image so it looked as though she were reporting from a nightclub. That is a bit unusual in itself, but the most interesting thing about this house turned ministudio is that for a year or so Marilyn Monroe lived there. The owner memorializes this with a painting and photograph of Monroe, which is the Hollywood equivalent of posting a sign saying, "George Washington slept here." Although "slept" takes on additional meaning in this context.

Walking back toward Ventura Boulevard, I pass an old Spanish-style home with a little second floor on one side. Donald O'Connor used to live here in the 1950s, and in that second-floor studio he gave tap dancing lessons. Among his neighbors sixty years ago were the actor Farley Granger and his parents. The Granger family had moved to Hollywood when Farley was young, and his mother enrolled him at

Ethel Meglin's dance studio, where Judy Garland and Shirley Temple had trained. His father found work at the California Department of Unemployment and at his office got to know Harry Langdon, a silent film star who was collecting unemployment. Langdon tipped off the father on a play that was casting in Hollywood; a young Farley Granger got cast and was discovered by talent scouts.

Granger's best-known roles were in two Hitchcock films, *Rope* and *Strangers on a Train*, both of which carried homosexual undertones in key relationships in the films, but they were so heavily buried by the Hays Office that Granger felt the films lost power. He himself was perfectly comfortable with his bisexuality, commenting in his memoir, "I was never ashamed, and I never felt the need to explain or apologize for my relationships to anyone … I have loved men. I have loved women." The list of both includes Ava Gardner, Arthur Laurents, Leonard Bernstein, and his longtime partner Robert Calhoun. Granger moved out of the house in Studio City years ago, but he left behind a caricature sketch he did of the cast and crew of one of his films. He made a sketch for every movie he worked on, and he stipulated—or at least requested—that this particular drawing, of *Small Town Girl*, with Jane Powell, Ann Miller, and Bobby Van, be left in the house. The owner has honored the request.

Walking back toward Ventura Boulevard takes me past the string of ranch houses that line every Studio City street. One lot has been newly cordoned off with a chain-link fence and covered in green plastic. I pause to mourn and curse. That green fence is the residential equivalent of the black shroud policeman toss over corpses: this home is marked for death. I peer through a gap in the chain link, and there is a cottage, a one-story Valley classic, with a white picket fence in front of the porch. A shingled roof is topped with a characteristic of a specific 1950s architect here, a tiny cupola with a birdhouse. There are trees on either side of the lawn, and I can imagine the interior because I have lived in these places: wood paneling from the 1940s, a timbered ceiling, wainscoting in the dining room, perhaps a wet bar in a corner of the living room, a fireplace, a kitchen that was remodeled in the 1980s with avocado-colored tile and ficus plants, but it's all now a little faded and shopworn.

A couple grew old in this house, and they are now ready for the Inn on the Boulevard nursing home, and they have sold their house to that damnable Israeli developer who buys Studio City homes every other week and immediately tears them down. One day a chain-link fence appears around a familiar neighborhood home; the next, the bulldozers come, and within a matter of hours the house is completely destroyed, the trees are removed with chain saws, and there is suddenly a lot that looks surprisingly large because the old ranch house stretched wide across perhaps a lot and a half, and in the back was a yard no one ever saw from the street, and now there is a gaping hole.

This hideous Israeli developer then throws up two enormous McMansions on this lot, all of the same design—two stories, the most prominent feature being a big garage door, all in the name of creating the maximum square footage, for in Los Angeles real estate the only thing that creates monetary value is square footage. For some reason, the only thing people/banks/mortgage companies care about is whether your home has 3,000 square feet or 4,000 square feet or, even better, 4,500 square feet. It doesn't matter what those square feet look like or whether the house is insanely too large for the lot and the neighborhood and looks like a cheap, crappy townhouse from Sylmar. It's just about the square footage, reducing the most essential principles of beauty and comfort to an economic equation measureable in terms realtors and Israeli developers can understand.

Then each McMansion is sold and the story is always the same: "I'm selling it to a doctor who has young children and will be here forever." Complete bullshit. It's always sold to someone who lives there for a year and then flips it for a higher price, and so what is charming about these little side streets in Studio City starts to look like the overdeveloped world of West Los Angeles, and something else is lost to the maw of commerce and the pursuit of a quick payday. Hollywood has always been a gold-rush city.

Now, placing my bile aside, I am strolling down Cantura, a lovely little street directly south of Ventura Boulevard, overarched by sycamore trees. The bowers of branches over the street makes it a great stand-in for a middle America small town, and while we lived there the house across the street served as the exterior for the popular comedy *Malcolm in the Middle*. One day I walked out and saw that house's yard had been stricken overnight, turning from green to completely dead and yellow. Thinking some strange catastrophe had befallen the lawn, some horrible horticultural epidemic that could be airborne and kill our lawn, too, I crossed the street to take a closer look. When I got close I realized that the art department had dressed my neighbor's lawn in an immense carpet of fake dead yellow grass—a bit of set dressing for an episode.

The whole town can feel like a back lot at times, with people's homes simply another version of Fox's New York Street. On most residential blocks in Studio City, you could assemble not only a set, but also the creative team to shoot something. Within a block of the *Malcolm in the Middle* house lived this assortment within the span of a decade: the director of *The Mack*, a working actor, two working ac-

Machiko Kyō, Marlon Brando, and Glenn Ford in Teahouse of the August Moon, *1956.*

tresses, a retired television star, a DP (director of photography), a film editor, and the son of Frank Zappa.

Many days on Cantura Street, I'd see an elderly man, rail-thin, nattily dressed, often with a scarf slung about his neck, pushing a shopping cart holding strange odds and ends. Some days I could identify a bag of groceries in the cart; sometimes it looked like odd pieces of scrap wood and debris; sometimes it appeared he was hauling away the kind of hoarder detritus that marks the unbalanced mind of a homeless man. But he wasn't homeless. He lived on Cantura Street in a small white house which, if one studied it closely, revealed a side wall above the garage that seemed to be formed of an ornate piece of carved wood. The kind of thing that might have come from a film set. Indeed, it had come from a film set. The owner, the gentleman with the shopping cart, took home bits and pieces of discarded set dressing from the films he worked on. He was Marlon Brando's makeup guy, Philip Rhodes.

We don't think about Brando having a makeup guy. Brando's passion for authenticity, his desire to reveal himself from the inside out as opposed to the British tradition of working from the outside in, would seem to denigrate makeup and the craft of disguise. We think of Brando growling in a makeup chair, squirming to be naked in front of the camera. But consider some of the roles he played: Sakini in *Teahouse of the August Moon*, Napoleon, Marc Antony, Zapata. All required serious makeup.

Makeup artists almost always have the most intimate relationship with actors. It only makes sense: they are the ones who stroke the actors' faces every morning, who insure that the women look beautiful, that the men don't age, who are the protectors of an image and nurturers of timeless beauty. Actors arrive in hair and makeup at ungodly early hours. They sit in a chair for perhaps a couple of hours or more, depending on the needs of the film. The actor sits there in a state that could be meditative, because there is really nothing to be done but be there in the moment.

Hair and makeup is always the best place to get gossip on any set. The women (and it must be said that most hair and makeup people are women) have a certain bounce; they are cheerful, and their mirrors are usually surrounded with photographs of their family or cast members in various stages of makeup and zany shots of crew members. They typically dress in outlandishly bright clothing, as if they feel compelled to wear a costume, too. For people who work all day with hair, their own hair is often carelessly tied back or dyed some impossibly bright color. They wear tool belts filled with the materials of their trade—brushes, makeup, and combs—and between takes, they quickly step in and pat down the actors, removing grime and sweat and endlessly spraying the hair so it doesn't change from take to take.

Philip Rhodes seemed different. Of course I only saw him from afar, as an elderly retired gentleman, usually with a silk scarf wrapped around his neck, wearing a suit jacket as he pushed his shopping cart down Cantura Street. I assumed he was gay—the makeup artist, the silk scarf around the neck—until a neighbor told me that Philip regaled him for hours with tales of his bedding women right and left. He then added this story:

There was a time late in Marlon Brando's life when everything was going wrong. His son Christian, in a drunken stupor of some sort, shot and killed the Tahitian lover of his half-sister, Cheyenne, and went on trial for murder. Brando was despondent. The neighbors on Cantura Street would see a long black limo come down from Mulholland Drive. It would first stop at the Baskin-Robbins Ice Cream store that used to sit at the end of Cantura Street. The driver would get out and purchase an entire tub of ice cream. Then it would pull up in front of Philip's house. Philip would emerge, get into the limo, and he and Brando would sit, eating ice cream.

The makeup artist as confidante. The person who has stroked your face lovingly for years and listened to you as you sat in the chair; that is the person Brando turned to in distress. Once again, a man seeks a place to sit and reflect on the world, sharing his thoughts with someone who never judges but only tries to make you beautiful. We could all use a makeup artist.

I turn a corner and arrive at Ventura Boulevard. I stroll past Art's Deli, "where every sandwich is a work of Art," a landmark since 1957, and largely unchanged since then. Its wide booths and open spaces, its extravagant pastrami sandwiches and chicken noodle soup have sustained generations of writers and producers, and it has provided a gathering spot for countless creative meetings, bitch sessions, and introductions. It is a day of mourning at Art's, as Art Ginsburg, who has owned and operated the place since the beginning, passed away on July 24, 2013. A little sign in the window commemorates his passing.

Art's has been home to innumerable industry lunches, conferences of producers and writers who come from the Radford Studio down the street, and every Thursday it is the home of the ROMEOs: Retired Old Men Eating Out. Principle among them is Abby Singer, a celebrated unit production manager. Abby Singer is the only person I know who has been memorialized in film parlance with a shot named after him. The final shot of a day of work is always termed the "martini shot," a jovial term that explains itself in the world of pre-sober filmmaking. The shot that precedes this, the penultimate shot of the day, has come to be known as the "Abby Singer," in fond respect for Singer's inclination to stay on schedule. An article in the Directors Guild of America publication *DGA Monthly* quotes Burt Bluestein explaining how the term came about:

> It all began when Abby was a 1st AD and people on the crew would ask him how many shots were left to do before lunch. Abby would answer, "We'll do this and one more." At the end of the day, when they asked what was to be done before the wrap, Abby would say, "This and one more, then we're out of here." The article continues with an explanation by Singer himself as to his logic in calling out the second-to-last shot: "In television, we would make maybe five

or six moves during the day—going from one set to another, or from one stage to another. Or we'd move from the back lot to a stage. I would say, "Fellas, we'll do this [shot] and one more and then we're moving." This would give the crew a chance to begin wrapping up their equipment or to call transportation for gurneys, so they'd be ready to get out quickly … I did it really to save time for the director. If we did it during the day, I could save 10 to 15 minutes each time we had to move. I could give the director another hour a day of shooting.

When the Studio City Improvement Association began embedding Ventura Boulevard's sidewalk with markers, the diamonds were implanted willy-nilly, with no place of honor or ranking system. This is the only explanation for how the plaque that originally sat directly in front of the entrance to Art's Deli commemorated *The Bob Crane Show*. Not *Hogan's Heroes*, but *The Bob Crane Show*. Most people no longer even know Bob Crane for his starring role in *Hogan's Heroes*. Rather, they know of his dispiriting end in a hotel in Phoenix, surrounded by the great passion of his life—pornography. His strange life and sad end was captured in the film *Auto Focus*, and to Google Bob Crane now produces such links as "So What Happened to the Bob Crane Sex Videos?" So, right out of the gate, Bob Crane was an odd choice to be commemorated. But even worse, to honor him in front of a revered Studio City landmark for his flop was sacrilege. Fortunately, the Studio City Improvement Association took the note, as we say in the business, and jackhammered out the offending diamond, replacing it with a crown jewel of Studio City production: *The Mary Tyler Moore Show* and its revered UPM and ROMEO, Abby Singer.

Saying a prayer for Art Ginsburg and all those ROMEOs in Art's, I walk back toward Laurel Canyon, passing the clothing store owned by William Shatner's daughter, past the Starbucks where every table is occupied with either someone writing a screenplay on a laptop or meeting about a project. I walk past the T-Mobile store, which used to be Buddy Brown Toys. Like many businesses that deal with objects that are not electronic, this great old toy store went out of business a decade ago. I still remember seeing a visitor book on the desk in which Marlon Brando had signed his name.

Within two blocks I come to CBS Radford, where Mack Sennett set up shop less than one hundred years ago. The timeline of Hollywood has been astonishingly short—Micky Moore knew Mack Sennett—and yet almost nothing remains of its physical history. It is the nature of the film industry that revolutionary changes come with startling frequency, leaving buildings, companies, and individuals ashore as the tide recedes, watching the boat they had been writing sail on to another destination.

The fact that *Sunset Boulevard* was made about twenty years after the silent era—and those actors and that world were viewed as complete dinosaurs, relics of some distant past—has always shocked me. It's as if the film stars of 1993 were obscure and forgotten by 2013. (For the record, the most successful films of that year starred Tom Hanks, Harrison Ford, Sally Field, Liam Neeson, and Denzel Washington, all still big stars.) But twenty years from today—in an entertainment landscape that now features video games grossing more than Hollywood films, and at the other end of the spectrum, overnight YouTube sensations with no staying power—twenty years hence, will all of this magical world of film and actors and sets and cameras and lights have evaporated into some new, piercing light that cleans Los Angeles of any past?

I walk home, past more diamonds in the Studio City Walk of Fame: *Secret Service in Darkest Africa*, a fifteen-episode serial about intrigue in Casablanca; the Orson Welles *Macbeth*; the TV series *The Adventures of Dr. Fu Manchu*, starring Glen Gordon; John Wayne in *Flame of Barbary Coast*; *Valley of the Zombies*; *Leave It to Beaver*; *Hill Street Blues*; John Steinbeck's *The Red Pony*; *Gilligan's Island*; *Scream III*. High art, low art, every human emotion and historical experience captured on film. The vast expanse of humanity wrestled into art by men and women working with scripts, cameras, actors, lights, and sets.

I should start digging now.

Notes and Sources

F. Scott Fitzgerald in the Butler's Cottage

A version of this chapter was originally published in the quarterly literary-culture magazine *Speakeasy*, Volume 1, Issue 4, March/April 2003, published by the Loft Literary Center, Minneapolis, Minnesota.

8 **"It's a gold rush, and like all gold rushes, essentially negative"** Matthew J. Bruccoli, ed., *Fitzgerald: The Love of the Last Tycoon: A Western*. The Cambridge Edition of the Works of F. Scott Fitzgerald. Cambridge University Press, 1993, p. 145.

8 **"Junior writers $300. Minor poets - $500 a week"** Robert Westbrook, *Intimate Lies: F. Scott Fitzgerald and Sheilah Graham: Her Son's Story*. Harpercollins, 1995, p. 16.

10–11 **Fitzgerald attempts to purchase his books for Sheilah Graham** Westbrook, pp. 167–169.

11 **"October 1938. FSF moves to cottage on the Edward Everett Horton estate"** F. Scott Fitzgerald, *A Life in Letters,* edited and annotated by Matthew J. Bruccoli. Scribner, 1995, p. 325.

13 **Edward Everett Horton's relationship with Gavin Gordon** Anthony Slide, *Eccentrics of Comedy*. Scarecrow Press, 1998, p. 65.

15 **"A young writer is tempted"** Westbrook, p. 416.

Jock Mahoney: The Thirteenth Tarzan

All quotations in this chapter are from a personal interview with Princess O'Mahoney, November 21, 2012.

Gidget, Alive and Well in Malibu

31 **"People don't realize I'm real"** Personal interview with Kathy Zuckerman, February 26, 2013.

35 **"… about my friends who lived in a shack on the beach"** From *Gidget* by

Frederick Kohner, copyright © 1957 by Frederick Kohner, p. ix. Used by permission of The Berkley Publishing Group, a division of Penguin Group (USA) LLC.

35–36 **"Boy, I sure felt right at home with the crew"** From *Gidget* by Frederick Kohner, copyright © 1957 by Frederick Kohner, pp. 37–38. Used by permission of The Berkley Publishing Group, a division of Penguin Group (USA) LLC.

36 **"On the other hand, a true story"** and **"Now my old man is a pigeon"** From *Gidget* by Frederick Kohner, copyright © 1957 by Frederick Kohner, pp. 3–4. Used by permission of The Berkley Publishing Group, a division of Penguin Group (USA) LLC.

41 **"There are no boundaries when you're out on a surfboard"** Personal interview with Kathy Zuckerman, March 20, 2013.

A Leigh Wiener Gallery

44 **"Remember, kid, tell me what you really think of them"** Personal interview with Devik Wiener, November 27, 2012.

44 **"I followed Bus, Barbara, Stanley, and Jeeb"** Leigh Wiener, *How Do You Photograph People?* The Viking Press, 1982, p. 14.

45 **"I guess they have her down in Santa Monica"** Interview with Devik Wiener.

46–47 **"I had a 250-millimeter lens and a 35-millimeter camera"** Transcription of a portion of the Leigh Wiener episode from the *Talk About* Pictures television series (1978–81).

48 **"How old are you, kid?"** Interview with Devik Wiener.

48 **"For many years I looked on movie writing as an amiable chore"** Ben Hecht, *A Child of the Century.* Simon and Schuster, 1954, pp. 466–467.

50 **"The sad thing about writing fiction"** William MacAdams, *Ben Hecht: The Man Behind the Legend.* Charles Scribner's Sons, 1990, p. 284.

52–53 **"For years I have tried to find the keys"** Jack Warner Jr. in the foreword to *Hollywood Be Thy Name: The Warner Brothers Story* by Cass Warner Sperling and Cork Millner. The University Press of Kentucky, 1988, p. xi.

54 **"Can you imagine? The president of Warners"** Sperling and Millner, p. 284.

54 **"He was what you saw. You knew what to expect"** Sperling and Millner, p. 333.

54 **"I hear my father now in the executive dining room"** Sperling and Millner, p. 335.

56 **Groucho on *Samson and Delilah*** Imdb.com, *Samson and Delilah* trivia.

56 **Groucho on Houdini** Transcription of a portion of *An Evening with Groucho*, a recording of a 1972 performance at Carnegie Hall (A&M Records).

56 **Once a priest approached Groucho** *An Evening with Groucho*.

58 **"There's a now, a was, and a gonna be"** Sid Caesar with Bill Davidson, *Where Have I Been? An Autobiography*. The New American Library, 1982, p. 271.

64 **They all socialized at Bogie's home** Gerald Clarke, *Get Happy: The Life of Judy Garland*. Random House, 2000, p. 335.

64–65 **"Fox … was like being in a big newspaper office"** Patrick McGilligan, *Backstory 2: Interviews with Screenwriters of the 1940s and 1950s*. University of California Press, 1997, p. 233.

The Dick Powell Show Grades Jack Nicholson: C+

All quotations in this chapter are from a personal interview with Norman Powell, May 7, 2013.

The Dick Powell Show script referenced throughout is "John J. Diggs." Stanley M. Kallis Scripts, Collection no. 0043, Special Collections and University Archives, University Libraries, Pepperdine University.

Mel Shavelson and the Last Bugler

The black binder of *The Little Bugler* notes and script is a personal copy, bought at a garage sale in November 2007.

86 **"[I was born] above the toy store"** Melville Shavelson, *How To Succeed In Hollywood Without Really Trying: P.S. – You Can't!* Bear Manor Media, 2007, p. 1.

86 **"That seemed to please him. There was no one to share my apartment"** Shavelson, p. 37.

87 **Lloyd tells this story about one of those uncles** Personal interview with Lloyd Schwartz, February 15, 2012.

90 **"I had reached the top of the mountain"** Shavelson, p. 216.

91–93 All quotations are from the black binder.

95 **"I know the world too well and the shortness of its memory"** Mel Shavelson Interview, Archive of American Television, interviewed by Karen Herman on April 6, 1999. Visit emmytvlegends.org for more information.

95–96 **"There are things that you can't explain their importance"** Mel Shavelson Interview.

SAMUEL GOLDWYN'S BIRTHDAY PARTY: A CONTACT SHEET BY LEIGH WIENER

100–101 **Screenwriter Philip Yordan remembers writing a scene** Patrick McGilligan, *Backstory 2: Interviews with Screenwriters of the 1940s and 1950s.* University of California Press, 1997, pp. 377–378.

101–102 **Phonevision** Samuel Goldwyn, "Hollywood in the Television Age." Originally published in *The New York Times,* February 13, 1949. Reprinted in *Hollywood Quarterly,* Volume 4, Number 2, Winter, 1949. Anthologized in *Hollywood Quarterly: Film Culture in Postwar America,* 1945–1957, edited by Eric Smoodin and Ann Martin. University of California Press, 2002, pp. 201–203.

104 **"It's sad to realize that today [in 1961]"** Harpo Marx with Rowland Barber, *Harpo Speaks!* Bernard Geis Associates, distributed by Random House, 1961, p. 224.

104 **Rose Hecht asked for silence** Marx with Barber, p. 392.

105 **"Mom and Dad were great friends with Elizabeth Taylor"** Carrie Fisher, *Wishful Drinking.* Simon & Schuster, 2008, p. 34.

106 **"[Not] just Elizabeth [Taylor] and Connie Stevens and Debbie Reynolds"** Eddie Fisher with David Fisher, *Been There, Done That.* St. Martin's Press, 1999, p. 18.

106 **"Frank [Sinatra] was the chairman of the board"** Jonathan Yardley, review of *Been There, Done That* in the *Washington Post Book Review,* September 26, 1999.

106 **"There were models and Playboy Playmates"** Eddie Fisher with David Fisher, p. 18.

106 **"I wanted to get my DNA fumigated"** Carrie Fisher, p. 67.

109 **"A breeze from San Francisco Bay"** George Jessel, *This Way, Miss.* Henry Holt and Company, 1955, p. 193.

110 **"You can't say that Jolson was an egocentric"** George Jessel, written for the now defunct United Press Hollywood, May 23, 1955.

111 **"When it came to shooting, he was letter-perfect"** Gary Fishgall, *Pieces of Time: The Life of James Stewart.* Scribner, 1997, p. 358.

112 **"I was scared shitless"** Milton Berle with Haskel Frankel, *An Autobiography.* Delacorte Press, 1974, p. 47.

113 **"It happens to be where Al Jolson was buried"** Bill Berle in James Barron, "Boldface Names: Correction Appended: Unrest Over Final Rest." *The New York Times,* March 29, 2002.

114 **"Milton Berle was an over-achiever and an under-achiever"** From "The Death of Milton Berle" at findadeath.com.

114 **"The problem with *Partridge*"** Susan King, "Classic Hollywood: Shirley Jones, still going strong." *Los Angeles Times,* May 13, 2009.

114 **"At the auditions, they introduced me to the lead actress"** No original source available.

116 **"I learned about life with Jack, about parties with Jack"** Shirley Jones, from an interview with Lynn Elbert for the Associated Press, July 2013.

118–119 **Farralone description** from "Farralone, The Legend" property listing at www.lynnteschner.com. Used with permission of Lynn Teschner.

Providence

122 **"In Los Angeles I have attended the serves of the Agabeg Occult Church"** Carey McWilliams, *Unknown California*, edited by Jonathan Eisen and David Fine with Kim Eisen. Collier Books, 1985, p. 209.

The Judy Garland Show

Much of this chapter is based on a personal interview with George Schlatter, March 21, 2013.

Notes and Sources

141 **"It was 1963"** Interview with George Schlatter.

142 **"[A] really repulsive human being"** Coyne Steven Sanders, *Rainbow's End: The Judy Garland Show*. William Morrow, 1990, p. 59.

143 **"Call me irresponsible"** Sanders, p. 65.

The Painter of Light

149 **"Imagine that 15 million American homes have a TV"** From personal notes for the pitch made to Lionsgate Films.

The Man Who Worked in Movies for Eighty-Four Years

159 **His daughter Sandy remembers the day** Personal interview with Sandy and Tricia Moore, November 13, 2013.

160 **"What is the role of the second-unit director?"** From the Frequently Asked Questions (FAQ) page of Micky Moore's website, www.mickymoore.com.

164 **His daughters remember working as extras** Interview with Sandy and Tricia Moore.

165–66 **"We were flying in James Gavin's Bell 47-J-2 helicopter"** Micky Moore, *My Magic Carpet of Films*. BearManor Media, 2009, p. 132.

169 **"It is always a great moment"** Moore, p. 248.

A Neighborhood Walk

173 **"I was never ashamed"** Farley Granger with Robert Calhoun, *Include Me Out: My Life from Goldwyn to Broadway*. St. Martin's Press, 2007, p. 41.

176–77 **"There was a time late in Marlon Brando's life"** Personal interview with Arla Campus, November 2012.

177–78 **"It all began when Abby was a 1st AD"** Burt Bluestein quoted in *DGA Monthly*, March 2002.

Photography Notes and Credits

Cover

On the set of the film *Career* starring Dean Martin, Anthony Franciosa, and Shirley MacLaine, 1959. Co-written by Dalton Trumbo, one of the Hollywood Ten, the film is about the blacklist. Micky Moore served as second-unit director. Courtesy Michael D. (Micky) Moore Papers, Collection no. 0117, Special Collections and University Archives, University Libraries, Pepperdine University.

Facing title page

Micky Moore with Mary Pickford in *Pollyanna*, 1920. Courtesy Michael D. (Micky) Moore Papers, Collection no. 0117, Special Collections and University Archives, University Libraries, Pepperdine University.

Introduction

W.C. Fields. Date unknown. George Grantham Bain Collection, Library of Congress.

Sebastian Cabot in a CBS publicity photo for the television series *A Family Affair*, 1967. Public domain.

Jerry Mathers in an ABC publicity photo for the television series *Leave it to Beaver*, 1961. Public domain.

Amanda Blake in a CBS publicity photo for the television series *Gunsmoke*, 1966. Public domain. The press clip with this publicity photo reads "PRETTY KITTY—Amanda Blake will appear prettier than ever in her role as Long Branch proprietress Kitty Russell when 'Gunsmoke' turns to color in its 12th season."

F. Scott Fitzgerald in the Butler's Cottage

F. Scott Fitzgerald from the June 1921 issue of *The World's Work*. Public domain.

F. Scott Fitzgerald portrait by Carl Van Vechten, 1937. Library of Congress.

F. Scott Fitzgerald and Zelda Fitzgerald in Dellwood, Minnesota, 1921. Public domain.

Edward Everett Horton. Date unknown. Public domain.

Photography Notes

Jock Mahoney: The Thirteenth Tarzan

Jock Mahoney as Tarzan in *Tarzan's Three Challenges*, 1963. Courtesy Princess O'Mahoney.

Jock Mahoney with his daughter, Princess, on horseback. Date unknown. Courtesy Princess O'Mahoney.

Jock Mahoney and his wife, Margaret Field, in Acapulco. Date unknown. Courtesy Princess O'Mahoney. This publicity photo came with accompanying text: "The fish nets of Acapulco make an interesting background for vacationing Jock Mahoney and his actress-wife Maggie, as they tour Mexico after Jock finished location work on Universal-International's 'Last of the Fast Guns,' the dramatic story of a manhunt filmed entirely in Mexico in color and CinemaScope with Mahoney, Gilbert Roland and Linda Cristal in starring roles."

Jock Mahoney as Yancy Derringer. CBS Network, 1959. Public domain. CBS offered this plug with its press photo for the *Yancy Derringer* series: "Jock Mahoney, who stars as swashbuckling Yancy Derringer, embraces Frances Bergen, his romantic vis-à-vis featured as Madam Francine, while his faithful Indian friend, Pahoo-Ka-Ta-Wah (X. Brands), looks on."

Jock Mahoney riding bareback. Date unknown. Courtesy Princess O'Mahoney.

Gidget, Alive and Well in Malibu

Kathy Kohner (Gidget) with her father, Frederick Kohner. Photograph by Alan Grant for the October 28, 1957, issue of *LIFE* magazine. Courtesy Kathy Zuckerman.

Kathy Kohner (Gidget) with surfboard. Photograph by E. Lenart. Courtesy Kathy Zuckerman.

Sally Field in an ABC publicity photo for the television series *Gidget*, 1965. Public domain.

Kathy Kohner Zuckerman (Gidget) in Malibu, December 2013. Photograph by Ken LaZebnik. Courtesy Kathy Zuckerman.

A Leigh Wiener Gallery

Leigh Wiener beside his photographs of Charles Laughton and Grace Kelly. Date and photographer unknown. By permission of Devik Wiener.

All other photographs in this chapter by Leigh Wiener. By permission of Devik Wiener.

Simone Signoret at the Academy Awards, 1960. Ben Hecht, 1956. Paul Newman, 1961. Jack Warner, 1963. Groucho Marx, 1966. Sid Caesar, 1962. Al Jolson at Jeanette MacDonald's party, Hollywood, 1948. George Burns, date unknown. Gregory Peck with Judy Garland at the Hollywood Foreign Press Awards, February 1955. Daryl Zanuck, 1963.

Elizabeth Allen's Garage Sale

John Wayne and Elizabeth Allen in a publicity shot for the film *Donovan's Reef*, 1963. Public domain.

Elizabeth Allen and Paul Lynde in an ABC promotional photo for *The Paul Lynde Show*, 1972. Public domain

Sergio Franchi in a publicity shot for the MGM film *The Secret of Santa Vittoria*, 1969. Public domain.

The Dick Powell Show Grades Jack Nicholson C+

Dick Powell publicity photo, 1938. Public domain.

Dick and Norman Powell, undated. Courtesy Norman Powell.

Jack Nicholson, *The Little Shop of Horrors*, 1960. Public domain.

Lee Marvin in a CBS publicity photo for the television series *The Twilight Zone*, 1961, "The Grave" episode. Public domain.

Mel Shavelson and the Last Bugler

Mel Shavelson, undated publicity photo. Public domain.

Cary Grant and Sophia Loren in a trailer from *Houseboat*, co-written and directed by Mel Shavelson, 1958. Public domain.

Kirk Douglas in a publicity photo from *Cast a Giant Shadow*, written and directed by Mel Shavelson, 1966. Public domain.

Photography Notes

Samuel Goldwyn's Birthday Party: A Contact Sheet by Leigh Wiener

All photographs by Leigh Wiener, 1962. By permission of Devik Wiener.

Samuel Goldwyn, Harpo Marx, Eddie Fisher, George Jessel, Jimmy Stewart, Milton Berle, Shirley Jones, Frank Sinatra (3).

Providence

A page from the writer's draft of a script for the NBC television series *Providence*, 2000. The episode was then titled "The Red Shoes"; it was later rewritten and produced with a new title. Script by Ken LaZebnik, handwritten notes by Ken LaZebnik from a session with show runner Bob DeLaurentis.

The Judy Garland Show

Judy Garland and Mickey Rooney on the set of *The Judy Garland Show*, 1963. Photograph by Leigh Wiener. By permission of Devik Wiener.

Judy Garland and Mickey Rooney in a publicity photo for the film *Love Finds Andy Hardy*, 1938. Public domain.

Judy Garland on the set of *The Judy Garland Show*, 1963. Photograph by Leigh Wiener. By permission of Devik Wiener.

The Painter of Light

Publicity photo of Thomas Kinkade. Courtesy The Thomas Kinkade Company, Windermere Holdings, LLC.

The author with Peter O'Toole on the set of *Thomas Kinkade's Christmas Cottage*, 2007. Courtesy Ken LaZebnik.

The Man Who Worked in Movies for Eighty-Four Years

All photos courtesy Michael D. (Micky) Moore Papers, Collection no. 0117, Special Collections and University Archives, University Libraries, Pepperdine University.

Micky Moore with Gloria Swanson in Cecil B. De Mille's *Something to Think*

Hollywood Digs

About, 1920. Micky Moore with William Boyd in Cecil B. De Mille's *The King of Kings*, 1927. Micky Moore (center) at a birthday party with young actors on the set of *The King of Kings*, 1927. Micky Moore with Murial MCormac in *The King of Kings*, 1927. Micky Moore directing Suzanna Leigh and Elvis Presley in *Paradise, Hawaiian Style*, 1966. Micky Moore with unidentified woman, late in his career. Photographer and date unknown.

A Neighborhood Walk

Farley Granger, undated publicity photo. Public domain.

Machiko Kyō, Marlon Brando, and Glenn Ford in a publicity photo for *Teahouse of the August Moon*, 1956. Public domain.

About the Author

Ken LaZebnik writes for television, film, and the theater. He shares story credit with Garrison Keillor for director Robert Altman's last film, *A Prairie Home Companion* (2006). LaZebnik wrote the Lionsgate film *Thomas Kinkade's Christmas Cottage*, released in 2008, starring Peter O'Toole and Marcia Gay Harden. His television writing has ranged from over twenty scripts for *Touched by An Angel* to writing for *Army Wives, Providence, Star Trek: Enterprise*, and the new series on the Hallmark Channel, *When Calls the Heart.*

He wrote three PBS specials for the series *In Concert at the White House* that were filmed in the East Room. These featured such varied performers as Broadway stars Patti LuPone and Jennifer Holliday and country star Toby Keith.

LaZebnik's plays have frequently premiered at Mixed Blood Theatre in Minneapolis, directed by founder and artistic director Jack Reuler. Their most recent collaboration was *On the Spectrum*, which premiered in November 2011, received a Steinberg/American Theatre Critics Association New Play Award citation in 2012, and had a successful run in 2013 at the Fountain Theatre in Los Angeles. Other plays by LaZebnik that have premiered at Mixed Blood include *Vestibular Sense* (2006), *League of Nations* (2002), and *Calvinisms* (1988).

His play *Rachel Calof*, adapted from the memoir of a Jewish homesteader in North Dakota, is a one-woman show starring Kate Fuglei. His play for young audiences, *Theory of Mind*, commissioned by Cincinnati Playhouse in the Park, has also been produced in Minnesota, Hawaii, and Michigan.

LaZebnik is the Founding Director of the Stephens College MFA in TV and Screenwriting Program (www.stephens.edu), a low-residency program based in Hollywood. For many years, he has taught screenwriting for the University of Southern California's Peter Stark Producing Program, an MFA program in the School of Cinematic Arts.

He lives in Los Angeles with his wife, Kate. Their older son, Jack, graduated from West Point, and their younger son, Ben, attends Columbia University.

Colophon

Cover and interior design
Lynn Phelps

Typefaces
ITC Anna Std
Minion Pro
Univers LT Std

Printed and binding
Versa Press, Inc.
East Peoria, Illinois

Published by
Kelly's Cove Press
2733 Prince Street
Berkeley, CA 94705

April 2014

Berkeley